INSIDE WRITING

DVD VIEWING GUIDE

W9-BLN-110.

This guide is designed to help professional developers use the DVD to lead teachers to new understandings about the teaching of writing. It may also be used to plan instruction for preservice teachers. And individual teachers will find suggestions and ideas here for ways to most effectively use, think about, and write about the DVD material independently.

INTRODUCTION

Donald Murray, who first taught Donald Graves to write, has said, "Teachers should write, first of all, because it is fun. It is a satisfying activity that extends both the brain and the soul. It stimulates the intellect, deepens the experience of living, and is good therapy. Teachers should write so they understand the process of writing from within. They should know the territory intellectually and emotionally: how you have to think to write, how you feel when writing. Teachers of writing do not have to be great writers, but they should have frequent and recent experience in writing. If you experience the despair, the joy, the failure, the success, the work, the fun, the drudgery, the surprise of writing you will be able to understand the composing experiences of your students and therefore help them understand how they are learning to write." (*A Writer Teaches Writing* 2003)

New as well as veteran writing teachers utilize the research of Donald Graves to guide instruction. His theories and research, epitomized by his germinal work in *Writing: Teachers and Children at Work* (1983) have informed the work of educational researchers for three decades. However, Don has noticed that most teachers continue to teach writing without writing themselves. Because teachers are reluctant to invest time in an approach they are not sure will make a difference in their teaching, they need to see why this component of writing teaching is valuable, how it energizes a writing workshop, and how to do it. If a picture is worth a thousand words, then video footage shot in today's classrooms is worth even more. This DVD demonstrates the power of teachers who write with their students and create workshops where the talk is writer to writer.

❧

How Is the DVD Organized?

There are seven components to the DVD and most include a demonstration lesson by Don.

GETTING STARTED covers the thinking and research that launched this project, as well as an explanation of how the DVD is organized.

CHOOSING A TOPIC offers six lessons that guide teachers in helping their students make good topic choices, including a sample of a teacher introducing a quick write prompt to second graders.

REREADING A TEXT deals with helping students find the heart of a piece of writing and using reading to teach writing.

USING DETAILS focuses on voice and details in writing while also zeroing in on the role of standardized testing in writing classrooms.

CONFERRING provides a fishbowl conference as a minilesson, individual and small group conferences with students, and teachers conferring with each other to get inside writing in different genres.

USING CONVENTIONS shows how teacher writing can help students to understand the decisions writers make about using conventions, and teachers to determine what students understand and what needs reteaching in a minilesson.

THE WRITER'S LIFE, which is the final section, includes an interview with Don Graves about his career in writing research, printable quick write prompts for the writer who prefers composing on a computer to using the notebook, samples of Don and Penny's writing used in the **Conferring** section, and biographies of the classroom teachers featured on the DVD.

❧

What Does the DVD Do?

The DVD allows teachers to watch colleagues work through the challenges of the apprenticeship approach with their students. It offers a choice of mentors to learn from and model. The four teachers featured on the DVD are at different stages in their own understanding of how to teach writing using their own writing. We suggest you use clips of each. The DVD allows teachers to leave the professional development workshop and continue learning at home by choosing which components most interest them in their own exploration of the DVD footage.

The scenes on the DVD can be viewed in any order. A teacher may access the section on adding detail to writing prior to a standardized assessment (since students are often cited for inaccurate use of detail in writing) or study the section on conventions with a colleague during planning time. The DVD allows teachers to determine importance according to their own professional development needs.

How Might a Professional Developer Start Using This DVD in a Teacher Workshop?

Both the introduction narrated by Don (see the **Getting Started** section) and the interview about Don's habits as a writer (in **The Writer's Life** section) present the principles used as a foundation for the *Inside Writing* program.

Getting Teachers Started with Writing

The most important preparation for any teacher of writing is to write. If you are leading a workshop on this subject, you should practice several quick writes so you have had recent experience writing and can draw on your own questions and discoveries made during the process of writing something you care about.

Before viewing, you might ask participants to write to these suggestions:

1. List five words that would describe you as a writer.
2. Narrow down that list to one word that best captures you as a writer.
3. Write for several minutes explaining why that word best describes your writing experience.
4. Write a brief scene where you capture a strong memory of one experience you've had as a writer.

Share these responses as a whole group, adding feelings and experiences to a wall chart that can help anchor the teachers in common experience before the workshop begins.

Next explore with teachers why they don't write with their students or on their own at home as, for example, they prepare to teach a particular genre. Again, record their reasons on chart paper so you can refer to them throughout your workshop.

Here are two common responses from teachers:

- *I'm not a writer. I don't write as well as the authors whose literature I bring into my classroom. Why would my writing be a good model?* As Don says in **The Writer's Life** interview, the teacher just needs to write a little bit better than the students. The teacher is the model of *process,* not product, and is the only one who can show the moves being made behind the scenes of a finished piece of writing.

- *I don't have time to write.* Don and Penny say that writing is the best preparation for teaching writing. Writing to quick writes just ten minutes a day for two weeks can bring about a real shift in understanding of what writers need, and bring greater clarity to the teaching of writing, which ultimately saves precious time.

We recommend that teachers do at least two quick writes during a workshop. These can come directly from the *My Quick Writes* notebook. We would also suggest that teachers use writing to reflect for a few minutes after viewing a section of the DVD. Writing is thinking and it will help teachers gather thoughts before sharing in discussion.

You could follow the writing with a viewing of a selection of scenes that show teachers engaged in teaching as writers. The following sections can help teachers see and feel the essential components of an effective writing workshop and spur productive discussion about teaching writing:

- Sue Ann shows students how she finds a topic in her writing notebook. (**Choosing a Topic:** "Write About What You Care About")
- Dexter rereads his historical fiction piece, looking for details that add to the moment. (**Using Details:** "Finding Your Voice")
- Sue Ann holds a fishbowl conference with a student so the class can learn the language of writers. (**Conferring**)
- Vicki talks about where she writes at home, demonstrating what a writer needs. (**Choosing a Topic:** "What Writing Is For")
- Don reviews his rereading process in a demonstration lesson. (**Rereading a Text**)
- Don and Penny confer about their writing (**Conferring**). *NB:* Before viewing this lesson, you should make and pass out copies of the texts used in this conference. (**The Writer's Life:** "Don's Writing" and "Penny's Writing")
- Sue Ann talks about the language writers use for a particular audience—like the reader of a standardized assessment. (**Using Details:** "Finding Your Voice")
- Dexter helps students find the heart of a quick write. (**Rereading a Text:** "Find the Pulse")
- Sue Ann shows how she uses conventions in her fifth grade memory piece. (**Using Conventions:** "Using Your Writing to Teach Conventions")

✺

FREQUENTLY ASKED QUESTIONS

Following are some common questions teachers ask during professional development workshops on the teaching of writing, and DVD connections to each answer.

WHAT ARE THE ESSENTIAL COMPONENTS OF WRITING INSTRUCTION?

Successful utilization of all the essential components in the following list depends on the lynchpin assumption that the teacher has had recent experience writing in the genre being taught. This founding principle is at the heart of every example on the DVD.

1. **STRONG MINILESSONS IN ALL AREAS OF CRAFT**
   - *Choosing a Topic*
     - Lucie creates a quick write response to artwork with her students. ("Quick Writes")

- Sue Ann uses her notebook for topic choice. ("Write About What You Care About")
- Vicki develops a memory from when she was in second grade. ("Modeling Topic Choice")
- Students talk about where they find topics. ("What Writing Is For")
- *Rereading a Text*
  - Sue Ann solicits help with a nonfiction piece. ("Guide, Don't Correct")
  - Dexter finds the heart of his quick write. ("Find the Pulse")
  - Lucie thinks aloud as she rereads her narrative with her students. ("A Writer's Responsibility")
  - Vicki uses what she's learned by reading to help her think through crafting choices. ("Read Well; Write Well")
- *Using Details*
  - Sue Ann and her students talk "writer to writer." ("Finding Your Voice")
  - Lucie's students help her find details for her text. ("Finding the Details")
- *Conferring*
  - Teachers confer with peers. ("Teaching Yourself to Share")
  - Students are guided in conferring well in individual conferences, small-group settings, and as a class. ("Teaching Your Students to Share")
  - The language of conferring in a fishbowl conference is modeled. ("Sue Ann's Fishbowl Conference")
  - A student uses conferences to help her with her writing. ("Conferences in Dexter's Room")
- *Using Conventions*
  - Teams of students highlight conventions in Sue Ann's writing. ("Using Your Writing to Teach Conventions")
  - Students discover how Sue Ann made conventions decisions in a text. ("A Conventions Minilesson")

2. **THE LANGUAGE OF WRITERS**
- Reading like a writer (**Rereading a Text:** "Read Well; Write Well")
- Teachers learning about writing from colleagues (**Conferring:** "Teaching Yourself to Share")
- Students developing the language of effective conferring: one-on-one, small-group, fishbowl (**Conferring:** "Teaching Your Students to Share," "Sue Ann's Fishbowl Conference," "Conferences in Dexter's Room")
- Thinking aloud while revising a writing piece (**Rereading a Text:** "A Writer's Responsibility")
- Showing your process (**Choosing a Topic:** "Write About What You Care About")

3. **THE TEACHER'S APPROACH TO TEACHING WRITING—INQUIRY AND DISCOVERY**
- Dexter, Sue Ann, and Lucie demonstrate how to find a topic by exploring ideas in a quick write. (**Choosing a Topic:** "Quick Writes")

- Sue Ann explores how narrative is used in a feature article while revising in front of her class. (**Rereading a Text:** "Guide, Don't Correct")
- Don thinks aloud as he explores a quick write entitled "On Chores and Toys." (**Choosing a Topic:** "Don's Demonstration")
- Dexter rereads his quick write looking for a pulse. (**Rereading a Text:** "Find the Pulse")
- Sue Ann thinks through ideas for her historical fiction piece with a student in a fishbowl conference for the class. (**Conferring:** "Sue Anne's Fishbowl Conference")
- Dexter considers which details to add and which to delete to improve focus in his historical fiction piece. (**Using Details:** "Finding the Details")

4. **THE ORGANIZATION OF THE CLASSROOM—MATERIALS, TIME, ETC.**
- How writing with students saves time (**Choosing a Topic:** "The Classroom Environment")
- Writing's place in the school day (**Choosing a Topic:** "What Writing Is For")
- How to manage a small-group conference (**Choosing a Topic:** "Write About What You Care About;" **Conferring:** "Teaching Your Students to Share")
- How sharing builds community in a classroom (**Choosing a Topic:** "The Classroom Environment")
- What students say about teachers who write (**Choosing a Topic:** "The Classroom Environment")

5. **LOOKING FOR CRAFT IN WRITING WE ADMIRE**
- Vicki shows the impacts her reading has on her writing. (**Rereading a Text:** "Read Well; Write Well")
- Don discusses the impacts his reading has on his writing. (**The Writer's Life** interview)
- Sue Ann refers to models of editorials in student magazines. (**Rereading a Text:** "Guide, Don't Correct")

WHAT IMPACTS CAN TEACHERS' EXPLORATION OF THEIR OWN WRITING HAVE ON THEIR WRITING INSTRUCTION IN THE CLASSROOM?

The teacher who writes raises expectations for all students. "I tried this," is a powerful invitation for students who admire and respect their teacher. "Texts have such a variety of structures!" is a marvelous opening for a minilesson in any genre under the direction of a teacher engaged in this discovery. As the teacher imagines the possibilities in structuring a text of her own, she models for students how to determine the best approach to telling a story, reporting on an experiment, or finding a focus for a piece of poetry. Likewise, as the teacher models revision, students consider new ways to reread and rethink their writing.

Watch how the teachers on the DVD connect with students through natural talk about their own writing processes. Building this community of writers begins with the teachers' own writing. These teachers model taking risks as a writer and allow the students to imagine doing the same.

WHAT ROLE DOES THE "LANGUAGE OF WRITERS" PLAY IN SUCCESSFUL WRITING WORKSHOPS?

Students need to learn how to articulate their understandings and misunderstandings about genre, form, voice, and conventions.

Talking about a piece of writing becomes an invitation for students to change the direction of a piece or to find the heartbeat at the center and write towards that center. Teachers give students the language to talk about writing with increasing sophistication through fishbowl conferences, strong minilessons, and thoughtful writing conferences. By modeling that talk in a fishbowl conference, students learn how to talk to each other in peer conferences.

Watch the peer conference on the DVD (**Conferring:** "Sue Ann's Fishbowl Conference") and listen to the language these fifth graders use to discuss their writing; it is not accidental. The teacher has demonstrated using this language by talking about her own writing in front of students. When students use a common language for writing, they are more likely to understand and learn from each other.

WHAT IS THE VALUE OF MAKING THINKING VISIBLE IN THE WRITING PROCESS?

A teacher's model of the decisions he makes as he composes helps students to compose with more confidence. Some students can imitate the process their teacher used in a genre. Other students might imitate the thinking and arrive at another way to nurture a text. The key component of a teacher's model is to scaffold writing decisions so that students know the kinds of questions they might ask in order to improve their own text.

HOW CAN A TEACHER USE THE MODELS IN THE DVD TO HELP TEACH STUDENTS TO BE SUCCESSFUL ON STANDARDIZED TESTS?

The teacher must model essential test-taking strategies in writing just as she models writing in any genre. Teachers show students how to write to a standardized prompt by composing writing to a test prompt in front of the students—talking aloud throughout the process so they can hear the thinking and the process as the teacher works to answer the question, weigh ideas, determine the best way to answer, and then work through the writing process: drafting, rereading, revising, editing.

Students must learn how to back up claims they make in their writing with details. The details should be relevant so that they truly support the claim. Again, the teacher can model rereading his own answer, looking for details that support the claims he has made. He can then take the process one step further, modeling how to improve test responses by deleting insignificant detail, helping students uncover where the text moves away from his intent and where sentences draw the reader away from his purpose.

❧

QUESTIONS YOU MIGHT ASK TEACHERS
AFTER VIEWING THE DVD

- How is your authentic exploration of your own writing evident in your teaching? How was it evident in the teaching in each of the classrooms on the DVD?
- What are some structures in your writing workshop that support lively and purposeful talk about writing? What structures in the DVD classrooms support that talk?
- What language do you hear your students using about writing in your classroom? What language is an echo of language you have used to teach writing? What language are they not using that you would like to see them develop and use in workshop?
- How can we help students become more effective problem solvers when encountering challenges in writing? What did these teachers do?
- In what ways can we help students learn how to reread their writing effectively to hear what doesn't make sense? How did these teachers accomplish this?
- What are some strategies to help students embrace revision? What kinds of talk and activity help students see revision as a way to nurture a text instead of 'fix it up' as if it were broken?
- How can we show students how writing develops an understanding of something we want to explore?

❧

SUGGESTIONS FOR SMALL-GROUP STUDY
FOLLOWING A WORKSHOP

The *Inside Writing* DVD offers more than two and a half hours of classroom footage, interviews, and commentary. Teachers will gain the most from meeting with a few colleagues (or even just one) and watching together, then reflecting on what they have seen. Reflections can be quick writes followed by discussion, or just thought processing at the end of a sequence.

INSIDE WRITING

HOW TO TEACH THE DETAILS OF CRAFT

Donald H. Graves
and
Penny Kittle

HEINEMANN
Portsmouth, NH

Heinemann
A division of Reed Elsevier Inc.
361 Hanover Street
Portsmouth, NH 03801–3912
www.heinemann.com

Offices and agents throughout the world

Library of Congress Cataloging-in-Publication Data
Graves, Donald H.
    Inside writing : how to teach the details of craft / Donald H. Graves and Penny Kittle.
      p. cm.
    Includes bibliographical references.
    ISBN 0-325–00729-2
    1. English language—Composition and exercises—Study and teaching (Elementary).
  2. Teachers as authors.   I. Kittle, Penny.   II. Title.
  LB1576.G72755 2005
  372.62′3—dc22   2005012174

Editor: Lois Bridges
Developmental editor: Alan Huisman
Production editor: Abigail M. Heim
DVD production: Kevin Carlson
Additional video production services: TLK Productions, Theresa Kennett, Producer/Director
Typesetter: Technologies 'N Typography
Text and cover design: Joyce Weston Design
Cover photography: David McLain Photography
Manufacturing: Louise Richardson

About the Cover:
Top: Penny Kittle (left) and two teachers featured on the DVD, Dexter Harding and Sue Ann Martin, coaching students on writing; *bottom:* Don Graves writing in his home office.

Printed in the United States of America on acid-free paper

09   08   07   06   05   VP   1   2   3   4   5

This project is dedicated to the memory of an inspiring colleague,

Melinda Puglisi, 1957–2005.

Melinda's love for students
and her passion for teaching writing
made an indelible mark on teachers and students
at John Fuller Elementary
in North Conway, New Hampshire for fifteen years.
She will be missed for many more.

"You'll be with me like a hand on my heart."   Drawing by Jeanne Puglisi

CONTENTS

APPENDIXES   98

ACKNOWLEDGMENTS

FROM PENNY

This project began with teachers. As I have traveled around the Mount Washington Valley over the last five years as a professional developer for the Conway School District, I have been inspired by the energy in writing classrooms where the teacher shares the process of writing with the students. Don and I have spent many afternoons talking about the impact of breaking down decisions writers must make in front of students, so that students can find their own path through a genre or a topic.

When Don and I began considering our presentation for the NCTE conference in San Francisco in 2003, we decided we needed video to capture some of the energy in a classroom when students see their teacher as a writer. Luckily, we called on a friend and talented producer, Theresa Kennett, who created a ten-minute clip, "When Teachers Write with Their Students." It was both inspiring and educational. We had a vision. Theresa's skill with editing and camera work helped us see what could be done with video. We are deeply appreciative. Theresa and her camera crew, including Ginny Kanzler, Bob Bernhardt, and Bill Edmunds, did most of the videotaping for this project. Their persistence helped us make the most of our time in classrooms and capture on videotape what we all love about teaching: students engaged in meaningful work. Thank you, Theresa. We couldn't have done this without you.

Our next step was to work with the professional and intelligent people at Heinemann. Lesa Scott, Leigh Peake, Maura Sullivan, Lisa

Fowler, Kevin Carlson, Alison Maloney, Pat Carls, David McLain, and Alan Huisman were instrumental in helping us realize this vision. They were patient and supportive as we all tried to get our hands around this project. Kevin's talent with script writing and editing molded our raw material into a teachable tool. Lois Bridges, our editor and friend, was a lifeline. As the project changed shape, Lois believed that the work was important, no matter what the obstacles. It was Lois who patiently followed our rabbit trails until we knew where we needed to be. It was Lois who waded through piles of paper helping us find the best focus for the text.

We spent most of our time on this project in two classrooms with outstanding writing teachers. Dexter Harding (Jackson Grammar School, Jackson, New Hampshire) and Sue Ann Martin (Broken Ground Elementary School in Concord, N.H.) are passionate and funny, focused and knowledgeable, flexible and daring. For months we were immersed in the hard work of teaching writing, but in very capable hands. We thank them both. Their students were terrific writers and articulate thinkers. Interviewing them was a pleasure.

We also videotaped for several days with Lucie Swain and Vicki Hill at Josiah Bartlett Elementary in Bartlett, N.H. On the brink of summer vacation they opened up their teaching to our cameras and disruptions. We captured much of what we love about this work and are indebted to them both. Ramie Coffey is the best of what it means to be a paraprofessional working beside students in the classroom. All three teachers created an environment for young writers that is worth emulating. We would also like to thank the principals at all three schools: Anne Kebler, Joe Voci, and Susan Lauze.

Don and I are in love with teaching. We take great energy from presenting to colleagues, particularly at the NCTE conference. Teachers ask insightful questions and constantly push our thinking. We read the work of our colleagues in journals, books, and articles and then discuss those things as we sit in Don's office looking out over the wilds of the White Mountains. We depend on the insights of our colleagues to fuel our own. Keep writing; keep publishing.

And finally, for our families we offer our greatest thanks. My husband, Pat, finally said one afternoon as I gathered binders and files to zip up to Jackson for an afternoon with Don, "You know, Penny, if he wasn't 74, I'd be worried. You spend more time with Don than you do with us." I thank Pat for his constant support of this work that drives me. He steadies me when I'm overwhelmed, holds me when I need a friend, and takes me to dinner (again) when I'm craving chicken caesar salad. I thank my delightful children, Cam and Hannah, for their coherent answers to my questions. I have pestered them both since they began writing to help me understand their process and how teachers help them write. They've answered patiently, saved their drafts, and then made me laugh with their stories and adventures. Lucky me to share my life with these three.

✺

FROM DON

I first met Penny Kittle after a reading at a bookstore in North Conway. She asked me to sign one of my books. Little did I know what the future held for the two of us. She asked me to give a talk at the high school and I completely forgot the assignment. As penance, I agreed to teach all of her classes for one day. She is a compassionate, knowledgeable teacher, and an outstanding writer. Penny has already published two books with Heinemann, *Public Teaching: One Kid at a Time* (2003) and *The Greatest Catch: A Life in Teaching* (2005).

I enlisted the help of my wife, Betty, to write many of the selections in the various genres. She gave excellent feedback as she went about the process of both writing and rereading. Betty reads all of my writing before it leaves the house. In this instance she entered the full life of collaboration as she wrote and reread her texts. We've come full circle as partners in writing.

Part I

The Teacher as Writer

When I began my teaching career in 1956 the school day was the same length as it is now. But the curriculum has expanded fivefold, interruptions have tripled, and assessment requires more attention than ever before. To say that today's teachers are pressed for time is a gross understatement. Nevertheless, when teachers compose texts of their own—texts they care about—during writing workshop, precious time is saved. Teachers reveal to their students the decisions all writers must make about every aspect of writing and demonstrate the skills that make writing clear and meaningful. *Inside Writing* asks you to use your own texts to teach writing.

It is unheard of for a math teacher not to show the art of solving problems on the chalkboard. An artist paints with his class, a science teacher illustrates the art of investigation and documentation, and a coach shows how she spreads her fingers to control a basketball. Good teaching means demonstrating the decisions and skills required to participate in the field of study or endeavor being taught. I invite you to take this journey with regard to writing.

I've been asking teachers to do this since 1983, when, piqued by Lucy Calkins' reasoning that short writing assignments allow an author to maintain better control and have a better chance of discovering his or her voice, I instituted a new course at the University of New Hampshire: Introduction to the Teaching of Writing. The point of the course was to help teachers become more comfortable with their own writing. Each day, for the first fourteen days, they identified two significant events and wrote about each for ten minutes, deliberately ignoring the writing censors they had internalized over the years, changing nothing and lowering their "standards": "Let your mind run, let all things in, but above all write without pausing." (This process closely resembles the rapid sketching young artists do as they try to capture a still life or a person running.) At first, my college students didn't enjoy this process at all. But by about the fifth or sixth "quick write" they discovered something interesting about themselves: they could spot a nice turn of phrase, a new sense of authority in their words. There was a voice inside them that was worthy of being shared.

Penny first heard about quick writes in a workshop with Linda Rief, and uses them in her high school classes to jump-start writing in all genres. Rather than asking students to write about a personal event, Penny offers a quick stimulus to their thinking by reading aloud a selection from literature, an article from the newspaper, a poem, or a short paragraph she's written herself. She then asks, "Okay, what struck you about what I just read? Write about it. Steal a line that you like or an idea you have an opinion about or just write what this piece made you think about. We'll stop writing at the end of five minutes." It is up to each writer to turn the passage to her or his advantage.

Heidi Noriega, one of Penny's students, had this to say about quick writes in her final reflection on a semester of writing:

> In quick writes our goal was to get our thoughts down on paper no matter how incoherent they seemed in our heads. This tool was vital in getting me to write, because I usually have writer's block for long periods, sometimes days. However, with the journal I was able

to write down my thoughts quickly without worrying what other people thought of my ideas or my writing. Most of my writer's block stems from fear: the fear that my essay will not have depth or will be incoherent. Surprisingly, when I went back to my quick writes I found many solid foundations for the writing pieces I created. My thoughts were not as incoherent as I had thought before I began to write. Journaling was the key to improving the quality and quantity of my prose this semester.

Quick writes became the basis for the other writing Heidi did that semester, and that's a point I want to emphasize: quick writes are *foundational* to a sound writing program; *they are not* the *program*. I freely acknowledge that there is no research supporting the case for and the place of quick writes in the writing curriculum. However, research shows that the following instructional techniques, all of which apply to quick writes, encourage better writing. The writer should:

SEE HOW TEACHERS USE QUICK WRITES IN THE CLASSROOM. (CHOOSING A TOPIC: "QUICK WRITES")

1. Write frequently.
2. Concentrate on main ideas.
3. Reread what one has written.
4. Organize one's writing.
5. Support claims with supporting details.
6. Use a distinct and recognizable voice.

This book is built on your own writing. You can't skip the writing part and just read this text. That explains the accompanying title, *My Quick Writes* notebook. You have work to do. The notebook also includes quick writes for children so that your students can write with you.

There are many reasons for you and your students to practice writing quickly.

1. **YOU LEARN TO WORK FROM A STIMULUS.** Writers need to get used to finding a personal response to a general stimulus. The writing prompts in standardized tests tend to be limited and

impersonal, but your students' work with quick writes will help them lasso a fundamental idea and develop it, then wrestle it to the ground.

2. **YOU LEARN TO GET OFF THE MARK QUICKLY.** With practice, writers get their ideas moving more quickly. Their first line moves closer to the emotional center of the piece.

3. **YOU BEGIN TO RECOGNIZE YOUR NATURAL SENSE OF ORGANIZATION.** Although the quick-writer is open to any and all thoughts, rereading the piece almost always reveals a natural structure. After you've written a number of quick pieces, you'll begin to see various organizational patterns. Sadly, many state, national, and local assessments superimpose a standard organization (the thesis statement and three supporting points, for example) on an assigned topic. Practicing quick writes helps you organize your thinking around meaningful topics in a variety of ways.

4. **YOU CAN IDENTIFY THE EMOTIONAL CENTER OF A PIECE AND PROVIDE SUPPORTING INFORMATION.** The most common response to student writing on a formal assessment is "lacks supporting details." Quick writes become the laboratory for teaching writing essentials.

5. **YOU CONNECT CONVENTIONS TO CONTEXT.** It is much easier to observe conventions when you care about the piece and your ideas are clear. Since quick writes lead authors to topics they care about, they will more likely attend to conventions as they write and refine the text. As you demonstrate writing with students, you will model decision making in terms of say, punctuation.

In Part II of this book, you'll reread some of your responses. Although there may be many ideas in one piece of writing, at the heart of the piece is your reason for writing it; somewhere you'll have shown, vividly, what that reason is. That's what you want to identify.

You'll also explore various genres: point of view; poetry (yes, poetry, even if you've never written poetry before); essays (beginning with a letter and then using it as a basis for an essay); and finally, fiction. I've saved fiction for last, because it's the most difficult: you have to create believable characters. I have a process that will help you and your students write fiction with greater control. And always, I'll write along with you and show how I mark up my quick writes in order to turn them into more substantial pieces of writing.

Part III, with the help of the accompanying DVD, shows you how four teachers use quick writes and their own writing in their classrooms to clarify the process of creating writing for their students. You can move between the book and the DVD, experimenting along with these teachers as you clarify and refine the way you teach writing.

CHOOSING A TOPIC: "QUICK WRITES"

Everyone has stories to tell, love letters to write, complaints to lodge, apologies to offer. Open *My Quick Writes* and scan the first few pages. Find a couple of ideas that appeal to you and write about each for about ten minutes. That's all you need to do the first day. Stretch those writing muscles and see what comes to the surface. Then, tomorrow and each successive day, do two or three more quick writes, until you've got about twenty or thirty of them.

Your life is far richer than any prompt in this book is likely to reveal. The prompts are provided for readers who may feel anxious about finding a topic and like assistance. Sometimes, too, a prompt leads you to things you had never thought to write about. I encourage you to explore your own interests and passions. Those areas will be far more interesting to you.

WATCH LUCIE USE A PIECE OF ART AS A QUICK WRITE PROMPT. (CHOOSING A TOPIC: "QUICK WRITES")

If you already have your own journal or another place in which you collect writing, do your quick writes there. (Perhaps you could share the quick writes notebook with a colleague and begin exploring writing together.) If you are more comfortable composing on a computer, you will find templates for each of the quick writes on the DVD.

THE WRITER'S LIFE: "PRINTABLE QUICK WRITE PROMPTS"

All right, it's time to dive in. And, remember, I'm cheering you on every step of the way!

PART II

LEARNING HOW TO
REREAD YOUR
WRITING

❧

I've always disliked rereading my writing. It feels good to write; why mar that feeling with a rereading? The voices of my former English teachers ring in my ears. I might find something shocking, some sorry use of words, or an irrelevant remark. I'm scared to death I'll dislike what I've written, and that means I'll have to do a major rewrite. Who has time for that? But learning to reread my work differently—looking beyond reading for errors—has made all the difference.

Writing encompasses many kinds of reading: reading your life to find writing topics, reading your writing plans and prewriting to decide on what to focus, reading your drafts to find the heart of the piece, and so on. I'll help you reread your quick writes by showing you how I coached my wife, Betty, through this important part of a writer's process.

So, take the pressure off yourself and look first for sections or words you like. Be kind to yourself. I have a long history of being ravaged by readers who don't know how to help me realize my own dream for the piece. Realistically, texts aren't good or bad; they are just unfinished and require more work. There is always more work to

Betty Graves, mother of five and grandmother to eight, worked as a nurse for many years. Her real interest is science. She toured New Hampshire as a docent making presentations in schools about whaling old and new, as well as served as a docent at Strawberry Banke in Portsmouth, NH. She is currently a trustee of the Jackson Town Library. As a reader, Betty consumes several books weekly in fiction and nonfiction. Don says, "Thanks to Betty's reading I have earned the equivalent of at least another master's and doctor's degree." Don and Betty have been married for fifty-one years.

be done beyond the first draft. As you refine your ability to reread, you'll get to the tough stuff soon enough.

I'm always hoping for a great first draft. It seldom happens—perhaps three times in thirty years! Penny and I have included some of our quick writes here and in the accompanying notebook to prove to you how rough the beginnings of our writing can be. Know that first drafts get better. You will find as you continue with the quick writes that your first drafts will improve markedly. Be patient. Crafting takes time.

We'll begin gently. I told you to lower your standards, remember? It's too soon for the nitty-gritty. Quickly reread the quick writes you've completed so far, and choose six pieces you'd like to revisit and possibly work on some more.

❧

REREADING TECHNIQUES

FINDING WHAT YOU LIKE: THE FIRST REREADING

Choose one of your six pieces and

1. **FIND A SENTENCE YOU REALLY LIKE.** Read the piece aloud and when you feel a perk of interest in what you wrote, underline that sentence.

2. **FIND THREE WORDS YOU LIKE.** These words may have surprised you or caused you to say to yourself, *that word just fits here.* Circle the words.

3. **FIND A PARAGRAPH OR SECTION THAT SURPRISES YOU.** A series of sentences in which you've uncovered and followed a thought that asks for greater attention or expansion. Put brackets [ ] around this section.

You may find that some of the text gets marked twice. Or, perhaps you won't mark anything at all. Some quick writes reveal little and are abandoned. This sifting through of ideas to find a topic is a natural part of the writing process.

To help you with your own rereading, let's look at my wife Betty's rereading of her quick write on woodchucks.

WATCH DON REREAD AND MARK UP A QUICK WRITE. (**REREADING A TEXT:** "DON'S DEMONSTRATION")

Woodchucks

Betty Graves

Woodchucks are small rodents about the size of a fat cat. They dig holes between boulders to make their homes. They then proceed to eat tender greenery.

That was all academic to me until I walked out into my (burgeoning) early summer garden to pick the peas that had tender-

SENTENCE I LIKE
That luscious . . .

WORDS I LIKE
(burgeoning)

SECTION I LIKE
[I had . . .]

crisply developed and were ready for my cooking pot. That luscious row was destroyed, gnawed off to stubby stems. I had woodchucks!

[I had labored over my garden: fall manure spreading, two rototilling occasions, raking, planning, planting, hands-and-knees crawling, weeding, sore back, dirty fingernails.] I was anticipating with delight the tasty crunch of fresh vegetables. But now this detestable rodent was enjoying my bountiful harvest.

I am furious. Let the war begin!

With this example fresh in your mind, choose another of your six pieces and again apply the three elements of rereading for things you like. If you wish, discuss the process with a colleague or friend. Was this rereading easier or more difficult than the first one? Why? If you feel the urge to rewrite, go ahead. Pull out a piece of blank paper or use some of the blank pages at the end of the notebook.

FINDING THE HEART OF THE PIECE: THE SECOND REREADING

Choose a new piece from one of the remaining four and

WATCH DEXTER SHOW HIS STUDENTS HOW TO FIND THE HEART OF A QUICK WRITE. (REREADING A TEXT: "FIND THE PULSE")

1. **LOOK FOR A SENTENCE THAT CONTAINS THE HEARTBEAT, THE PULSE, OF WHAT YOU WANTED TO SAY.** This is your wish for the piece, what it is most about. Underline that sentence.

2. **FIND THE LINES THAT MOST SHOW WHAT THIS PIECE IS ABOUT.** Put brackets [ ] around that section. It could be the sentence that contains the heartbeat. Here's an example. Suppose the heartbeat of a piece is that Frances is disorganized. The following lines *show* that disorganization: *Frances opened her purse hunting for her driver's license. She tossed papers, loose change, car keys, and a host of other items, like wrapped candy and throat lozenges, onto the tabletop.* "It must be in here somewhere," she bellowed.

3. **FIND TWO SENTENCES THAT ARE LEAST ABOUT THIS STORY OR SUB-JECT.** These sentences are farthest from the heartbeat. Enjoy drawing light lines through those sentences.

4. **READ YOUR PIECE ALOUD. FIND FOUR WORDS THAT YOU JUST LIKED THE WAY THEY SOUNDED TO YOUR EAR.** Circle those words.

Again, to help you, look at the following example.

A Photo I Remember

Betty Graves

There we are in a 1938 black-and-white Kodak shot: my sister, confident and smart at 8; my baby brother, cute and creeping at 10 months; and I, the assertive and (prickly) middle child at 6. We are playing tiddlywinks for the benefit of my father. He takes a yearly photograph of his family in October which he then turns into a picture Christmas card in his bathtub darkroom upstairs. We have already done several takes, getting each child's face into proper perspective, correcting for my baby brother's (erratic) motion as he disturbs the game pieces on the board and puts them into his mouth. Finally, all is ready. My father's final instructions are to look down at the game as if we were really playing it. He gives his order twice. [My sister obeys and rattles the pieces on the board so that baby, Ray, also looks down.

I decide it's better to look at the camera.] The photo is well (composed,) my father chose it, after all, from his many negatives. I am (preserved) forever, in my mind, as the independent, difficult, middle daughter. That designation has stuck in my head ever since.

> **HEARTBEAT**
> I am . . .
>
> **MOST ABOUT**
> [My sister]
>
> **LIKE THE SOUND**
> (prickly)

If you wish, try applying these rereading techniques to one of your earlier selections. You may not be able to find some of these elements in your rereading—they may not be present. This does not mean your piece is not good. It's just that the ways of rereading don't necessarily apply to every piece of writing. If you decide to add, replace, or delete text as you reread, do it. Listen to your piece and make changes that you feel are important.

LOOKING AT DETAILS: THE THIRD REREADING

Choose one of your remaining three pieces and

1. **FIND THREE VERBS THAT ARE PRECISE ('KICKED' INSTEAD OF 'HIT,' PERHAPS, OR 'VAULTED' INSTEAD OF 'JUMPED').** Underline those verbs. If you wish, find three more verbs that are not as precise and circle those with dotted lines.

2. **FIND A SENTENCE THAT IS SIMPLE AND DIRECT THAT CONTAINS NO CLAUSES.** Sometimes simple sentences sum up or say very clearly what a piece is about. Double underline that sentence.

3. **FIND THREE NOUNS THAT REPRESENT ADDITIONAL INFORMATION YOU HAVE INCLUDED OR COULD INCLUDE.** Circle them. Worlds of knowledge lurk behind certain nouns. For example, in writing about fishing for striped bass, I mentioned reaching into the *tackle box* for a new lure. But a *tackle box* contains so many other things as well. The same could be said of a *sewing box,* which contains spools of thread, scissors, measuring tape, various sizes of needles, or an assortment of buttons and zippers.

Once again, look at the following example to help you get the idea.

I'm from Boston

Betty Graves

I'm from Boston, that cultured, historic seaside city filled with universities, museums, theatres, and parks. The Boston of my day, 1930 to 1954, had much of the downside of slum life, triple deckers, run-down, rambling wooden houses broken into many apartments on streets where you must be watchful if you were a young girl at night. My home was in the Boston suburbs with tall trees, land still undeveloped, wide fields with blueberries in summer and sledding in winter. A famous (arboretum) was at the bottom of our hill with showy displays of massed lilacs and daffodils each spring.

My mother took her parenting responsibilities seriously and took her children to <u>marvel</u> at (museum) artifacts. We were taken to see the glass flowers at Harvard. I stood in awe under the whale skeleton <u>suspended</u> from the ceiling at the Natural History Museum. I thrilled to the dancing and costumes of *The Student Prince* at the Opera House. I rode the streetcars, elevated trains, and (subways) of the city observing its people and neighborhoods. We took the ferry across the harbor to Nantasket while I watched its huge pistons <u>churning</u> down in its engine room. I went to the circus with elephants, trapeze artists, and silly clowns. <u>What an enriched childhood I had.</u> My city, Boston, was the perfect jumping-off point!

PRECISE VERB
marvel
SIMPLE, DIRECT SENTENCE
What an . . .
THREE NOUNS
(arboretum)

Consider applying these rereading techniques to one of the remaining two pieces you chose originally.

THE URGE TO REWRITE

Go back to one or two of your pieces that you have reread and marked up with various pens and pencils. Take some time now, relaxed time, and rewrite just enough so that you have a sense of satisfaction. Here are some experiments you might try.

1. Take your best sentence or the sentence in which you show what the piece is about and move it up to lead off the piece. Reread what you've written out loud. What effect does that have on the rest of the paragraph or the whole piece? Many of us write our way into a piece with preliminary thoughts, but

WATCH DON MOVE THE HEARTBEAT SENTENCE TO THE START OF HIS SECOND DRAFT IN A WRITING CONFERENCE WITH PENNY. (SEE THE CONFERRING SECTION)

readers don't need these early scribbles of "getting in"; they want the meat or action right away.

2. There is a natural chronology to most events. Take another look at your piece to see if you are observing the natural order of things. Ask, *what does the reader need and when does the reader need it?* Writing is much like teaching. You are teaching your reader what you know about an incident or conveying some content that has a natural chronology. It may mean you'll delete some details and add others.

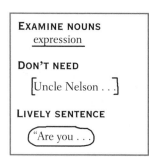

WE LEARN THIS NATURAL ORDER IN OUR READING LIFE. WATCH HOW TEACHERS CONNECT READING TO WRITING IN **REREADING A TEXT: "READ WELL; WRITE WELL."**

A MORE ADVANCED REREADING

1. Examine your *pronouns* (*he, she, it, our,* etc.). Make sure every pronoun refers to a solid noun. Are your pronouns clear?

2. Check your *adjectives.* Reread the nouns to which they refer. Can you get rid of the adjective by changing the noun?

3. Check your *adverbs* that modify verbs. (Adverbs may also modify adjectives or other adverbs.) Can you use a more precise verb that doesn't require the adverb?

REREADING AND REWRITING

Read this piece that I wrote about my Uncle Nelson.

Uncle Nelson's Photo

Don Graves

Uncle Nelson is just coming up the <u>boat runway.</u> He has that <u>expression</u> on his face, a quizzical one in which his next words might be, "Who the hell are you?" or "Did you clean that boat?" An old felt hat is on his head and a stub of a <u>cigar</u> in the side of his mouth.

EXAMINE NOUNS
    expression

DON'T NEED
    [Uncle Nelson . . .]

LIVELY SENTENCE
    ("Are you . . .)

We don't have many pictures of Uncle Nelson but that one is my favorite. [Uncle Nelson rented boats and my brother and I had to take care of them. He not only rented the boats but built them.

In the background of the shot are the actual boats he built with oak and pine timbers. The boats were twelve to fourteen feet long with a good wide 5.5' beam and tough enough to stand the misadventures of boat renters.]

Uncle Nelson usually assaulted his visitors with questions. One time I brought my friend Will Saydah down to the Point for a visit. When I introduced him to Uncle Nelson, Nelson said, pointing to me, "Are you as dumb as he is?" Of course, he'd follow his query with a raspy laugh.

On other occasions he'd burst into a gathering of women and start singing a sea chantey at the top of his lungs, "Oh, Nelson, why do you sing those songs?" But secretly I think they liked his irreverence. They didn't often hear profanity and deep down enjoyed his raunchy humor.

Back to the photo. Nelson wore rubber boots that cut slightly below his knees. He needed those boots as he was around boats and water so much. His shirt was open but I can't remember if the sleeves were short or long.

Behind the underlined nouns stands much lore that I could introduce into this character sketch, though it might be distracting.

BOAT RUNWAY: Long two-by-fours stretching from the boathouse into the water, even at low tide. Boats arrived or departed using those boards. In the evening all the boats were pulled up onto the grass and then sent down the runway again when fishermen arrived to take the boats out the next morning. Each evening we'd tie a bowline knot from the painter to the tow rope to haul the boats up.

EXPRESSION: Nelson's expression was created by his felt hat, cigar, and challenging eyes. They all went together.

CIGAR: The cigar was just an unlit stub that nestled in the corner of his mouth. He didn't really smoke the cigar as much as just like to feel it there. It was part of his facial makeup.

Let's reread the piece again looking for the heartbeat. "Uncle Nelson usually assaulted his visitors with questions" isn't the heartbeat per se; the assault is shown in the evidence supporting that observation: "Are you as dumb as he is?" There's life in that line. I underline it.

Which section is farthest from who Uncle Nelson is as a personality? The last paragraph doesn't fit. It's a factual description; it doesn't capture who he is. This section has to go. (Of course, sometimes a section that diverts from the main point serves some other function in a piece and stays in.)

Let's examine the first paragraph again. The photo captures Uncle Nelson coming up the boat runway. Right away I look for a good verb that shows the way he is moving up the runway. *Saunter* may not be the right verb, but my uncle was lanky and loose-jointed, so I think *saunter* works. I also want to continue showing my uncle before I let him speak—that's the natural order—so I zero in on him from the shoulders up: *He wears an old felt hat and a stub of an unlit cigar is tucked in the corner of his mouth.* The first paragraph now reads:

Uncle Nelson saunters up the boat runway. At eighty-three he is lanky and loose-jointed. He wears an old felt hat and a stub of an unlit cigar is tucked in the corner of his mouth. His keen expression assaults friends or newcomers alike: "Who the hell are you?" or "Did you clean that boat?" 🦌

A good verb is difficult to find, but verbs are worth paying attention to. When the nouns are rich with meaning, as *boat runway, cigar,* and *expression* are, good verbs will usually follow. A strong noun is secretly looking for a precise verb to extend its meaning. Writers write with nouns and verbs, and they use adjectives and adverbs sparingly.

By now you've got the idea, so let's move beyond rereading personal narratives and look at how to reread some other genres.

✺

POINT OF VIEW

I was visiting a second-grade classroom on a cold New Hampshire morning in February. Children came in from the playground, their cheeks red with cold and their eyes wild with anger and indignation. I asked what the trouble was, and they replied, all together, "The fifth grade is taking over the playground—kicking our balls—keeping us off the jungle gym—pushing our faces in the snow."

I said, "Come over here; let's get some of these protests and details down." I listed their grievances on chart paper but drew a line down the center.

"Okay, now I'm going to make a list from the point of view of fifth graders. Tell me what I should write from their point of view. Look through their eyes and tell me what I should write. Pretend you are fifth graders."

The look on their faces said they thought I'd gone over to the other side: fifth-grade opinions were not to be entertained! I asked, "So when they did these things to you, they didn't have any viewpoint?" Again, sullen silence. Eventually, we carved out a fifth-grade viewpoint but it was tough going.

Such scenes are replicated at all levels of American life. There is only one point of view—mine or ours! Let's try to shake free from that egocentric stance. Once again, I'm going to ask you to do some quick writes, just ten minutes at a time. In each case, you'll be introduced to a number of people who have different ways of looking at a single issue. Your task is to take on the point of view of each person, first person, present tense. Here's an example of what I mean:

> My name is Mark. I strongly object to having a reading textbook imposed on me. There are some good stories and authors in there, but there is just nothing like having a good library in the room to which children have easy access. I have over five hundred books for them to read. There is nothing like sustained reading in a book in which a child is really interested to give him the fluency he actually needs. Reading programs don't get into real books. ✺

> My name is Eliza. Frankly, the reading textbook is a godsend. I'm just starting out as a teacher. I don't have a very good library in my room. If the kids need books, I send them to the school library. This allows me to have reading groups in which we can read, discuss, and do follow-ups to what we are reading. I'm also pretty shaky on the skills the children should be learning. I'm confident that the new reading program will help me and the children. Maybe later on I can provide a broader range of choices for the children. ✺

QUICK WRITE PROMPTS ARE ALSO AVAILABLE IN **THE WRITER'S LIFE** SECTION ON THE DVD.

Now it's your turn. Turn to the point of view quick writes in the notebook and try a few of the exercises.

REREADING POINT OF VIEW

There are some specific procedures for rereading point-of-view pieces (many of these pieces are also essays, so you're learning how to reread essays as well).

1. Circle four emotionally laden words, especially nouns. Circle them even if you like the sound of them.

2. Underline one sentence that contains the heartbeat of your point of view.

3. Put numbers (1, 2, 3, etc.) next to the facts that support your point of view.

4. Consider moving your heartbeat sentence to the very beginning of the piece.

5. Consider the effect that that sentence has on the entire piece.

6. Put brackets around any narrative contained in your short piece.

7. Draw light lines through sentences that are *farthest* from your heartbeat line.

Don't panic. Here are some examples to help you get a feel for what I'm after. Here's Betty taking one point of view about town planning.

Town Planning in a Mountain Valley Village

Betty Graves

In our small village there is a simmering controversy over town planning and zoning. [We have recently seen a (grotesque) rambling hotel go up in our town center. Its turrets and jutting windows cut out the mountain view and (obstruct) access to a wild river. Many townsfolk were angry after the fact. Another group has organized serious planning so that a pattern of development can be in existence before another (ruinous) change occurs.]

Those in favor of planning see how we could use an antique barn that sits downtown, now useless. It could be moved close to the school to provide library, auditorium, and cafeteria space at a lesser cost than new construction. They favor moving the major roadway and access to the bridge so that the intersection is safer

HEARTBEAT
In our . . .

NARRATIVE
[We have . . .]

EMOTIONALLY LADEN WORDS
grotesque

FACTS SUPPORTING POINT OF VIEW
①
. . . center. Its . . .

and the town can have a larger unified area for post office, town hall, school, library, and several stores. They③ wish to close certain parts to commercial development and restrict any building in watershed areas. This planning group has held several townwide information gatherings and forward looking meetings. They will continue to push their agenda on to selectmen's meetings and over the next few years to a decisive town meeting for actual vote of funds.

Now Betty takes the opposing point of view.

Expensive Changes Are Not Needed in This Lovely Valley

Betty Graves

ARGUMENTS
①
. . . we will . . .

EMOTION WORDS
crushing

HEARTBEAT
. . . if we start . . .

The opponents of these extensive town changes are first concerned with money issues. Changes are fine except we① will find them very expensive. Our crushing tax burden can only increase if we start moving barns, town hall, and the main road. We are an independent, do-it-myself, live-free-or-die, New Hampshire mountain people who do not want or need federal help. Our② traditions are so important. Our quaint red, shingled library is a beloved landmark, something we remember from contented childhood days. Moving it would change our town center badly. It's ridiculous to think that anyone would build or develop the steep rocky roadside area we need for watershed.

Furthermore, what is happening to property③ rights and an individual's ability to use his land as he sees fit? If I am unable to sell or leave my land to benefit my grandchildren because of zoning, my rights are unjustly④ curtailed. We don't need our town prettied up by a planning board organized by rich newcomers to our town. Jackson is a gorgeous location that has been a magnet for tourists for over 140 years. Change just for appearance⑤ is not a good thing. We are a charming place. Let's leave a good thing alone.

Experimenting with point of view can help you anticipate questions a reader may have in an expository essay. Even in narrative or fiction, the writer considers the views of other characters in the story. Practicing to write from an alternative point of view can help you reach new understanding about your topic.

AFTER WATCHING HER TEACHER DEMONSTRATE, A STUDENT CONSIDERS AN ALTERNATIVE POINT OF VIEW FOR HER STORY IN **REREADING A TEXT: "A WRITER'S RESPONSIBILITY."**

POETRY

Poetry is filled with surprises. I remember the first poem I consciously wrote. I said to myself, "I think I'll write about the feeling of running free on a beach." As a former English major, I worked hard to get in alliteration, metaphor, the full repertoire of figures of speech. I was really out to impress an audience. The poem was breathy, shouting at the reader, "Here I am! Here I am! Aren't you impressed?" In short, the sounds of poetry were present but my loud presence distracted the reader. The poem didn't make much sense.

Poetry is big thinking in a short space. And nothing is too small for a poem. Most poetry is just plain talk that uses simple nouns and verbs to penetrate a subject in an interesting way.

Poetry can be a great way to teach writing, because the texts are concentrated and easy for students to focus on. All the rules that apply to poetry are basic to the other genres as well.

1. A poem can have but one focus.
2. The basic structure is communicated through nouns and verbs.
3. There is a key line that shows what the poem is about.
4. A poem expresses deep feeling that is made evident in the details the author supplies to support the main point.
5. Poets use all of the senses to create vivid detail.

One day I sat in my study pondering some writing. As usual a thick, plastic pen was in my mouth. My teeth were gently making impressions on the plastic. I suddenly thought, "I've been doing this for a long time. In fact, it goes way back to Miss Jones in first grade, who kept telling me to take things out of my mouth." The following spoof emerged as I listed all the things I chewed in first grade.

In First Grade

Don Graves

In first grade
Everything is edible;
Soft, primary pencil wood
To run my teeth down

Like corn on the cob.
Second course is paste
During reading while
Miss Jones's yellow eye
And green smile catch
Me in mid-mastication
Of a primary chairback
During story time;
Fresh erasers nipped off
The end of borrowed pencils
Or brown art gum erasers
Offered as hors d'oeuvres
From the art supply cabinet;

Then I reach for the fragrant
Golden ends of Delores Gallo's
Hair hanging over the back
Of her chair and on to the books
On my desk.

At recess rawhide webbings
In a baseball mitt, then green

Crabgrass pulled just so
To gnaw white succulent stems
Like salad at Sardi's.

Who needs warm milk
And graham crackers smelling
Of the janitor's basement
At the Webster School
When we're already seven courses in?

Check out some poetry starters in the *My Quick Writes* notebook. Once again, choose five or six ideas that are closest to you in sense and feeling and give it a whirl. Ignore those that don't connect with you. Here's an example of mine to get you started.

I Am the Person Who

I am the person who
Always knows the time,
The day, the date,
If I am early or late.

People call to ask
How long it takes
To drive to Stowe, Vermont;
Or, what's the flying time
To Chicago, or Los Angeles?

As I write, I select details and mark them off into short lines. This may not seem poetic to you, but I'll work on sound and craft a little more when I rewrite. Notice that I try to end each line with a noun or a verb so that I and my reader will have an image of an object or an action. Also notice that I write in first person and present tense so I and my reader will feel the immediacy of the poem.

Here's another example of how to get started. This prompt, like the previous one, lends itself to a poem in the form of a list. A list poem is the simplest yet easiest way into poetry.

The Shopping List

I open the freezer compartment
And search for a hamburger patty;
There is no hamburger,
And I don't ordinarily eat hamburger.
But the other day I sank
My teeth into a sesame seed
Hamburger roll loaded with relish
And medium rare meat;
A shiver of delight swept
Over me and memories
Of meat cooking on a grill,
The smell running up my nose,
Made me add hamburger to my list.

Here's one more example to help you on your way.

Picking Up the Mail

My mailbox was created
In another era and time
When junk mail wasn't invented,
When only letters
Graced the tiny window.

Now I reach and wrench
The magazines, countless catalogs,
And annoying newsprint,
Splashing best food buys
In three colors.

I tug, pull, and curse the nameless
People who add my name
To the computer mailing list.

I asked my wife if she would take a few of these starters and write them as poems.

"And you want me to take just ten minutes to write them?" she asked.

"Yes," I said, "That way you won't try to pull in all the things you were taught in English class about reading and writing poetry. I want you to write as if you've never written a poem before."

"As a matter of fact, I haven't."

"Just the person I'm looking for," I said.

Betty was a nursing student fifty years ago but did well in her English courses. I know that she writes with excellent detail (see her earlier piece about the Christmas photo her father took). I gave her one more guideline: end your lines with nouns and verbs. This is what Betty wrote, in just thirteen minutes.

WATCH DEXTER TURN A QUICK WRITE INTO A POEM AS A DEMONSTRATION FOR HIS STUDENTS (**REREADING A TEXT: "FIND THE PULSE"**)

The First Time I Flew in a Plane

Betty Graves

The first time I flew in a plane
My father was the pilot of a bouncy Piper Cub
Motor roar, faster and faster.
Blue sky lifting, wind's roar,
Glass lake, houses and cars become
Children's toys.
Crazy world whirling.
Unreal angles, stomach turning.
Ground returns with blessed firmness.
Dad smiles. My heart wonders.

WORDS I LIKE
bouncy

MY VOICE
Crazy world

HEARTBEAT
Crazy world whirling

I asked her to circle three words she liked, and she circled *bouncy, whirling,* and *blessed.* I then asked her to circle a line that sounded like her own writing, and she circled "blue sky lifting, wind's roar." And finally she underlined the heartbeat: "crazy world whirling." Seeing that she had found the task difficult, I said, "I'd like you to write a second draft. Try not to sound like a poet, even up your lines, and try to end them with solid nouns and verbs." Here is her second draft.

> The first time I flew in a plane
> My father, the pilot of the bouncy Cub
> The motor roars, breathless speed
> Blue sky lifting, wind's roar
> Glass lake with azure glitter
> Houses and cars a child's trinket
> Crazy world whirling
> Earth angles, belly lurches
> Ground returns with blessed weight.
> Dad smiles. My head still airborne.

It's hard to describe the feeling of a first flight, but Betty manages to get good endings to her lines. The most difficult task is to avoid adjectives and adverbs that spice up the line but take away from *showing.* Betty tried another draft.

> The first time I flew in a plane
> My tense fingers clutch the seat.
> The motor roars. Breathless speed.
> Tumbling space under, blue sky lifting.
> Incredible the glass lake,
> Houses are children's trinkets.
> A crazy world whirls.

The world tumbles.
My belly lurches.
Ground returns with solid safety.
My Dad grins; my heart still airborne.

I pointed out a solid line, "My tense fingers clutch the seat," but offered a suggestion: "If your fingers were clutching the seat, you could probably dispense with *tense.*"

Betty was struggling between describing flight and capturing her relationship with her father. It meant a lot to her that she could share this first flying experience with him. She trusted him utterly. Still, I suggested that maybe it would be better just to focus on her flight.

Betty then said, "You know, I'm getting sick of this poem. Why don't I move on?"

I heartily agreed. Things were becoming too complicated. Sometimes a change in topic is just what a writer needs.

Here's Betty's next poem, written in twelve minutes.

Spiders

Betty Graves

Mottled legs hooking into their webs,
Sinister eyes probing for flies.
On guard, hanging with pendulant
Bellies over my head.
The fall spiders, grown fat
Over summer, are about
To lay myriad eggs for more
Mottled legs next spring.

My pitiless broom finds
Their lair.
Pulled to the deck, <u>they make</u>

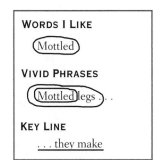

WORDS I LIKE
Mottled

VIVID PHRASES
Mottled legs . . .

KEY LINE
. . . they make

> Greasy, yellow yolk stains
> Under my vengeful heel.

The three words she liked were *sinister, mottled,* and *vengeful.* For the line that sounds most like her style, she circled "mottle legs hooking into their webs." But where is the heartbeat? I told her that the last line sounds more like her than the first one and it gives the feel of the entire piece. We had a good laugh over that, and then Betty wrote a second draft:

> Mottled legs hooked to webs,
> Sinister eyes probe for flies.
> With dread I watch
> Their pendulant bellies hang.
> The fall spiders, grown fat over summer
> Will soon lay myriad eggs
> For more mottled legs next spring.
>
> My pitiless broom
> Finds their den.
> Thrown to the deck, they make
> Greasy yellow, yolk stains
> Under my vengeful heel.

Betty is able to focus fully on her spiders, a simpler subject than flying. The good news is that she is applying so much of what she learned in writing the first poem. Her nouns and verbs are much more precise and therefore do not require adverbs and adjectives to support them. As Betty explained, laughing, "Spiders have always gotten to me ever since I went out to the woodpile to bring in wood for the stove. I must have been about ten years old. I was carrying about nine stove-length pieces when I spied a huge spider right on top. I let out a yell and tossed all the wood into the air."

Now it's your turn. Go to the Poetry section in *My Quick Writes* and try a few.

🦢

LETTERS INTO ESSAYS

We have the mistaken notion that essays are distant and dispassionate. It ain't necessarily so. Essays are meant to convince the reader that he'd better get off his butt and get busy doing what the writer wants. At the very least, the reader ought to change his mind about some issue worth thinking about.

Shirley Brice Heath caught my attention a few years ago when she said, "My research convinces me that the origin of the essay is the letter" (personal conversation). A letter is written to one person and expresses a passionate idea about something. When the letter is meant to convince more than one person, it is shaped differently— the pronouns change and the language becomes more universal—but with no less passion.

Let me show you what I mean. The other day I was taking a Delta flight from Cincinnati to Little Rock, Arkansas, and I overheard a counter attendant complaining about the flight delay. What I heard concerned me, and later I wrote a quick email to a friend:

Dear Steve,

I was sitting in my seat waiting for a plane to take off recently when the pilot announced, "We have a slight delay, but we'll be leaving in about twenty minutes." I thought, "Well, it must be the heavy rain in Arkansas." But when the counter attendant passed the manifest to the pilot he said, "There will be more delays in the future, because we are so understaffed. People are quitting left and right."

I know the airlines are having trouble making a profit. United Airlines can't get a loan to stave off bankruptcy. Delta is losing money and this means later and later departures. All because of the need to cut personnel costs. And I'm wondering what recourse passengers have to ensure they'll make their flight connections.

Steve, you fly for Delta. How do you interpret these things? Any insights?

Best,
Don Graves

There is feeling in this letter I wrote to Steve, shaped by my own personal concern about making my connections on future flights. Taking the letter as the basis for an essay, I use more universal language but continue to write in first person.

The other day I was waiting for my flight to take off from Cincinnati to Little Rock, Arkansas. Just five minutes before scheduled departure the pilot announced a flight delay of twenty minutes. At the end of the twenty minutes I found out why. The counter attendant delivered the passenger manifest to the pilot, saying, "I know this is late but we are understaffed. People keep quitting, and in the future these manifests are going to get later and later."

The airline industry is in trouble. Fuel costs have soared, and the airlines just haven't recovered from the 9/11 tragedies. United Airlines is in bankruptcy, and most of the major airlines are losing money. We used to get meals. Now there are none, even on a coast-to-coast flight. The greatest expense over and beyond the cost of fuel is personnel. Most employees have taken big pay cuts, and now ground crews are being cut, beginning with people at the desk. So, my flights will be late, but I'm wondering when there will be a whittling away of personnel who keep the plane safely in the air. 🦋

Notice that I begin with the same story. Essays often include first-person narrative, either at the beginning or later on. A personal narrative tugs at readers' emotions; it's a hook that makes them want to continue reading.

In paragraph two the tone shifts from *I* to *we*, in a brief presentation of facts about the airline industry. I need facts to back up my initial reaction to the counter attendant's statement. I end with general concern on behalf of all other airline passengers: "I'm wondering when there will be a whittling away of personnel who keep the plane safely in the air."

For this group of ten-minute quick writes, first write a letter to a friend whom you feel shares your point of view. (Seven possible topics are suggested in the *My Quick Writes* notebook.) This friend needs to be a real person in your life. You don't need to send this letter, but the text should be true to the contours of the friend's personality. Knowing that this letter might go to him or her will make the writing flow more easily. Then write an essay on the same subject. (Of course, you may have issues closer to your heart than the ones suggested in the accompanying notebook. If so, write your letter and essay on a blank page.)

I asked my wife to choose a topic of interest to her, write a ten-minute letter to a friend about it, and then convert the letter into an essay. The issue had to be one about which she could muster some degree of passion. Here is Betty's letter.

DON MAKES THE SHIFT FROM NARRATIVE TO ESSAY IN **CHOOSING A TOPIC:** "**DON'S DEMONSTRATION.**"

Dear Susie,

You have always been interested and active in public affairs so maybe you'll be sympathetic when I share my concern about the upcoming elections. These presidential debates bring all the issues to a boil. I'm so upset by what may happen to our social security system. How do you manage to sleep well at night with so many worries about our country?

Over our working years, we complained about how much was deducted from our paychecks for social security. Now, as retirees, those social security payments have become a substantial part of our dependable monthly income. We want it to continue for our children and grandchildren. Evidently some want to privatize retirement plans, allow some of the deductions to be invested by the individual herself. The government is spending the social security payroll tax for current expenses and not investing in the future, so real trouble looms ahead. I want to vote for the party that will fix social security not abandon it.

Are you concerned about this? Do you see any possible solution? Looking forward to your ideas.

Betty

REREADING THE LETTER

I then asked Betty to reread her letter following these basic guidelines (reread your own letters using these same guidelines).

1. Where do you connect with the person receiving the letter, betray knowledge of a personal nature?

2. Do you address the person as caring, smart, and knowledgeable?

3. What are the details of your concern? Number them.

4. Is there an urgency or concern? Underline the words that show this.

5. Is there a passive voice in your letter ("one might suppose that")? How active is your voice in laying out your concern?

6. Do you return your attention to the person receiving the letter?

7. What pronouns do you use in the letter?

8. Where is the heartbeat? Underline that sentence.

Here's how Betty marked up her letter in answering these questions. (She confessed that she was writing to a composite friend and agreed that choosing one friend and writing more personally to her would have made the assignment a little easier.)

Dear Susie,

(You) have always been interested and active in public affairs so maybe you'll be sympathetic when (I) share my concern about the upcoming elections. These presidential debates bring all the issues to a boil. (I'm) so upset by what may happen to our(1) social security system. How do you manage to sleep well at night with so many worries about our country?

Over our working years, (we) complained about how much was deducted from our paychecks for social security. Now, as retirees, those social security payments have become a substantial part of our dependable monthly income. (We)(2) want it to continue for our children and grandchildren. Evidently some want to privatize retirement plans, allow some of the deductions to be invested by the individual herself. The government is spending the social security payroll tax for current expenses and not investing in the future, so real trouble looms ahead. I want to vote for the party that will fix social security not abandon it.

Are (you) concerned about this? Do (you) see any possible solution? Looking forward to your ideas.

Betty

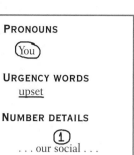

PRONOUNS
(You)

URGENCY WORDS
upset

NUMBER DETAILS
(1)
. . . our social . . .

HEARTBEAT
I want to vote. . .

COMPOSING THE ESSAY

I then asked Betty to write a ten-minute essay based on her letter. She laughed and said, "Are you kidding? Essays are a lot tougher than letters. It is going to take me at least fifteen minutes to write an essay."

"Okay, I said, "Take the time you need."

Here's Betty's essay.

Social Security, Yes or No?

Betty Graves

As I watch George Bush and John Kerry debate the burning issues of the 2004 election, I hear their differing views on the faltering social security system. Mr. Bush would privatize part of the FICA withholding payments from our paychecks, thus leaving even less funds available for the growing number of future retirees. Disciplined people will use the extra funds wisely, but some will neglect to invest, thus living as poverty-stricken elderly.

Mr. Kerry promises to fix social security, selecting a bipartisan committee to decide what must be done: raise the retirement age or increase FICA withholding tax or decrease the amount of monthly payments.

The social security system in America, begun under the Roosevelt Administration, has lifted our elderly out of poverty. It is one of the few programs that genuinely help the poorer population. Besides the expected retirement income, it provides some insurance against sudden incapacitating health disasters and death. We do not want two Americas: one rich and self-sufficient, the other poor and angry. We need an America that cares about all its people. A viable social security system is a requirement in a just America. 🦌

REREADING THE ESSAY

Here are the guidelines Betty used as she reread her essay (use them as you reread your own).

1. Put brackets around the content you carried over from your letter.

2. Did you write in first person (*I*)? Second or third person?

3. Where do you begin to address a broader audience (*we, they*)?

4. Number one side of the argument 1, 2, 3; use Roman numerals (I, II, III) for the other side of the argument.

5. Underline the sentence in which you express your opinion after weighing the evidence.

6. Underline the adjectives and adverbs in your opinion line. Are these words strong enough to justify your claims?

7. Put check marks where you sense you need more information, which you would research and insert in a subsequent rewrite.

Here's how Betty marked up her essay in responding to these directions.

Social Security, Yes or No?

Betty Graves

As I watch George Bush and John Kerry debate the burning issues of the 2004 election, I hear their differing views on the⌈faltering social security system.⌉ Mr. Bush would⌈privatize⌉part of the FICA withholding payments from our paychecks, thus leaving even less funds available for the growing number of future retirees. Disciplined people will use the extra funds wisely, but some will neglect to <u>invest,</u> thus living as poverty-stricken elderly.

Mr. Kerry promises to fix social security, selecting a bipartisan committee to decide what must be done: raise the retirement age or increase FICA withholding tax or decrease the amount of monthly payments.

The social security system in America, begun under the Roosevelt Administration, has lifted our elderly out of poverty. It is one of the few programs that genuinely help the poorer population. Besides the expected retirement income, it provides some insurance against sudden incapacitating health disasters and death. We do not want two Americas: one <u>rich and self-sufficient,</u> the other <u>poor and angry.</u> We need an America that cares about all its people. <u>A viable social security system is a requirement in a just America.</u>

CONTENT FROM LETTER
 [privatize]

ONE SIDE OF ARGUMENT
 ... FICA witholding

OPPOSITE SIDE
 ... funds available ...

ADJECTIVES
 invest

OPINION SENTENCE
 A viable social ...

Essays take time and require a lot of rewriting. When teachers reveal the process by writing their own texts, the mystery surrounding the writing of essays is penetrated. Most teachers give essay assignments that are too lengthy and don't require nearly enough rewriting or digging for information. Letters to the editor are short, and most op-ed pieces in the newspaper don't exceed five hundred words.

*

FICTION

I used to think that writing fiction meant I needed to come up with a good plot to keep my readers interested. Unfortunately, the belief that fiction is all about plot is a common misconception.

Reading the *Paris Review,* I ran into this statement by Neil Simon: "Only recently did I discover that my plays didn't really take off until the main character wanted something, and wanted it badly." Fiction is really about *character.* It is about showing characters wanting things, having aspirations they hope will be fulfilled, or wanting a different life from the one they are living at the moment. Of course, it isn't long before all this "wanting" produces tough choices, and negative and positive reactions from others. Usually, the main character learns something about life itself.

Of all the genres fiction is the most difficult for me to write. I have to create human beings, with all their strengths and weaknesses. And these traits have to be believable. Writers of fiction often ask each other, "Yes, but would he really do that?" "Would she really just leave everything to run off with that bum?" The writer has to provide enough information for the reader to make an informed decision.

Some time ago I did a study of children's written fiction (*Experiment with Fiction,* 1989). I learned that very young children's fiction is all about plot. The main character is secondary. But when children begin reading good young-adult fiction, around the fifth grade, they learn about characters and are able to produce them with some dimension.

When I write fiction, I have to know a great deal about my characters in order for them to be able speak and react to what other characters say. To some degree, I choose people (or composites of people) I have known, then place them in a setting with a problem.

Not long ago I made an attempt at a novel whose protagonist was Joshua Tripp, a young boy of ten, whose father is captain of a scallop dragger out of Fair Port, Massachusetts. Joshua's father owns a sperm whale's tooth etched with a scene of a seaman harpooning a big whale. The father says to him, "Some day this tooth will be yours. The story of how this scene got on here is written somewhere in my letters." But the boy wants the tooth today, not some day. I had to consider the boy's point of view, try to *become* the boy in essence, and wonder what he knows. But the real question is what do *I* know? I had to know something about scalloping, scrimshaw (the etching on the whale's tooth), and also old-time whaling to be able to connect to the reader.

READING YOUR WORLD FOR CHARACTER TRAITS

I cannot choose characters or scenes for you to write, because I don't know what you know. But I will take you through the process of getting to know a character and then sketching him in.

First, I think about people I know: my daughter, a neighbor, a friend, or my father. I choose my father, and on a blank piece of paper create a table of things I remember about him.

Dress, Body	Sayings, Foibles	Knows	Common Scenes
Baseball cap, brim bent	"When did you leave? How was the traffic?"	Baseball	Weeding on hands and knees
One-day stubble	"Sox are playing well."	Hybridizing glads	Walking up from the garden
Paunch		Blueberries	
Open shirt	"Have a new glad cross."	Fertilizer	Sitting in favorite chair in living room facing TV
Tight belt	"There's too much rain." / "It is terribly dry."	Administration	
Trousers soiled			
Shoes caked in dirt	"Newspaper come yet?"		Drinking coffee at kitchen table and reading newspaper
Shuffles when walks as if hips hurt	"Need any money?"		

Next, I take these traits and choose a fictional situation in which to put my father. Even though my father died in a nursing home at age ninety-three, I decide to imagine a different, earlier passing. Although the list of traits is long in my workup of Dad, like a cartoonist, I choose just a few of them to fit the situation. My underlying questions are, How did Dad die? How does his death reveal his character?

Face Down

When Dad didn't come up for his midmorning coffee and doughnut, my mother said, "You'd better go check on your father."

We'd always said that if Dad were to drop dead sometime, we'd find him in the garden. The garden was his quiet place away from the bustle of the house where the phone rang and Mother would be on his case about wearing his Sunday trousers to weed. Dad didn't care much about clothes. They kept him decently covered.

I went out the back door and gave a good yell, "Dad!" Now, the garden is only a hundred feet or so off the back door and he should have answered. But then, he's pretty hard of hearing, so maybe his head was low down in his gladiolas. Or maybe he was deep in thought pondering his next cross.

I crossed the back lawn and under the giant English elm to the edge of the garden. I scrutinized the near thousand glads all in rows, carefully weeded. Strange that he was so careful about an immaculate garden in case visitors should come, yet he cared so little about his own person. What first caught my eye was the far end of the rows where about a dozen gladiolas had apparently gone over.

An alarm went off; my heart started to race as I quickly went to that end of the garden. Dad was face down in the dirt as if he'd lurched suddenly to the right, knocking over the glads. I reached to touch him, turned him slightly. His face was as peaceful as if he'd just decided maybe this was the best place to go. ✤

REREADING FICTION

Rereading fiction is all about seeing whether I've kept my promises to the reader. Is the evidence there so the reader can say, "Yes, I think I know why she said that, why he did that"?

WATCH SUE ANN COACH HER STUDENTS IN USING DETAILS: "FINDING YOUR VOICE."

I reread the first line: *When Dad didn't come up for his midmorning coffee and doughnut, my mother said, "You'd better go check on your father."* I don't see this as a statement of alarm but of the need to see if Dad has been working too hard. Mother always said that Dad worked way beyond his physical capabilities. She knew his hips hurt and sometimes he had trouble standing up and maybe would have trouble getting up to the house.

My next line, therefore, is off base: *We'd always said that if Dad were to drop dead sometime, we'd find him in the garden.* I'm jumping the gun. I need Mother to speak again—to say *why* she wants me to check: *Your father works too hard, way beyond what his hips can stand. I remember the day I went out there and he just couldn't even stand up.*

But let me do this more methodically. Here are some questions to ask when rereading fiction.

1. *Where do you introduce the problem into the story?* I underline "You'd better go check on your father."

2. *What evidence is there to support raising the problem?* The big question is, why isn't Dad back to take his coffee break? I circle the evidence.

3. *How is the problem solved?* Double underline the course of action. I head out to try to find Dad. I ponder a series of thoughts: Why is Dad always in the garden? Why is he careless about his clothes? Why does he like to show visitors a well-weeded garden? I reveal my father in my journey out to the garden.

4. *What new evidence is introduced so the reader goes, "Oh-oh"?* This is the turning point in the story. Put brackets [ ] around your turning point. I spot the gladiolas leaning over and I don't see my father.

5. *What is the series of actions/reactions?* Underline the reaction of the main character to the unfolding event. Put double brackets [[ ]] around this section. I find my father face down. How do I react to that? Is he breathing? Is he struggling? I guess I would say "Dad" again.

Here's how I marked up my story.

Face Down

When Dad didn't come up for his midmorning coffee and doughnut, my mother said, "<u>You'd better go check on your father.</u>"

We'd always said that if Dad were to drop dead sometime, we'd find him in the garden. The garden was his quiet place away from the bustle of the house where the phone rang and Mother would be on his case about wearing his Sunday trousers to weed. Dad didn't care much about clothes. They kept him decently covered.

I went out the back door and gave a good yell, "Dad!" Now, the garden is only a hundred feet or so off the back door and he should have answered. But then, he's pretty hard of hearing so maybe his head was low down in his gladiolas. Or maybe he was deep in thought pondering his next cross.

I crossed the back lawn and under the giant English elm to the edge of the garden. I scrutinized the near thousand glads all in rows, carefully weeded. Strange that he was so careful about an immaculate garden in case visitors should come, yet he cared so little about his own person. What first caught my eye was the far end of the rows where about a dozen gladiolas had apparently gone over.

An alarm went off; my heart started to race as I quickly went down to that end of the garden. Dad was face down in the dirt as if he'd lurched suddenly to the right, knocking over the glads. I reached to touch him, turned him slightly. His face was as peaceful as if he'd just decided maybe this was the best place to be.

| PROBLEM INTRODUCED |
| "You'd better . . . |
| EVIDENCE |
| . . . (the garden) . . . |
| PROBLEM SOLVED |
| I crossed . . . |
| TURNING POINT |
| [What first . . .] |
| REACTION OF MAIN CHARACTER |
| [I quickly . . .] |

And finally, here's my rewrite.

The Way It Was Supposed to Be

When Dad didn't come up for his midmorning coffee and doughnut, my mother said, "You'd better go check on your father. I went down there last week and he couldn't even stand up."

The garden was his quiet place away from the bustle of the house where the phone rang and Mother would be on his case about wearing his Sunday trousers to weed. Dad didn't care much about clothes. They kept him decently covered.

I went out the back door and gave a good yell, "Dad!" The garden is only a hundred feet or so off the back door and he should have answered. But then, he's pretty hard of hearing so maybe his head was low down in his gladiolas. Or maybe he was deep in thought pondering his next cross-pollination.

I crossed the back lawn and under the giant English elm to the edge of the garden. I scrutinized the near thousand glads all in rows, carefully weeded. Strange that he was so careful about an immaculate garden in case visitors should come, yet he cared so little about his own person. What first caught my eye was the far end of the rows where about a dozen gladiolas had apparently gone over.

An alarm went off; my heart started to race as I quickly followed a row to that end of the garden. Dad was face down in the dirt as if he'd lurched suddenly to the right, knocking over some prize glads. I shouted, "Dad!" as if to wake him from sleep. I reached to touch him, turned him slightly. His face was as peaceful as if he'd just decided maybe this was the best place to be. ✺

Now it was Betty's turn. I asked her to choose a person she knew and create a table of things about this person like I did about my father. Her list included the following people.

1. **MOTHER AT AGE NINE.** I don't know an awful lot about what she did. I'd have to surmise a lot, because my grandfather died before I was born. A story I might tell about her father's homecoming from teaching in Europe just before the First World War doesn't seem too interesting.

2. **AUNT NELLY AT AGE EIGHTY.** She was an interesting character. She lived a lonesome single life. I'd be speculating too much. I don't know what to have her do.

3. **MY NEIGHBOR RACHEL AND HER DOG LIZZIE.** I know Rachel very well and could flesh out her character. I don't like her dog. I

guess I wouldn't want her to see what I'd write. I don't think I have anywhere to go with a story line.

4. **MR. RENTERIA, A MAN AT THE PRISON.** He is an interesting character. His looks are different. The poor man is always looking down. He struggles so in reading. I could imagine something that happened to him in jail or before he came to jail.

5. **ELLEN CRESPO, WHOM I DRIVE TO HER CANCER TREATMENTS.** I'll choose her because I know her quite well. We've talked a lot during our drives. When I think about her, I think of a story line about how she got her cat.

Betty's chart looked like this.

Dress, Body	Sayings, Foibles	Knows	Common Scenes
Stiff wig	"Get into the right lane here."	Cooking	Purse over arm, moving deliberately
Gray coloring	"My daughter says . . ."	Daily routines	Unwraps a throat lozenge
Some jaundice	"Before my husband died, we used to . . ."	Speaks German	Bends over her flowers at front door
Deep gravel voice	"When I get home I'll have those potatoes I cooked with onions."	Family life and child rearing	Bright smile when she sees me at Wal-mart
Clothing smells of moth balls	Loves her home and predictability	What her cat likes	Adjusts elastic waistband of her trousers
Matronly, sags around waist	Doesn't want to be a burden	Flowers and gardening	Takes frequent swigs from water bottle for her dry cough
Absolutely unremarkable		How to balance her budget to include medical bills and cancer prescriptions	
Reddish brown skin at front of neck			

And here is Betty's story.

Ellen Decides

Betty Graves

Morning was never a very good time for Ellen these days. Her gray face with hints of jaundice in the eyes greeted her each day in her bathroom mirror. She could tell her dry hack never let up. Even the cough drops didn't help much any more. It was lonesome being a widow and alone all winter in this trailer park. Even so, she knew she was lucky to have this doublewide, solidly built with big windows and a good heating system.

Her breakfast of cornflakes over, she forced herself to continue her usual routine. She jammed her arms into her puffy jacket, took the umbrella, and started out on her morning walk into a drizzling rain.

As she slogged down her road, her neighbor, Janet Kelly, waved to her from the doorway and stepped out onto her porch piled with boxes.

"Ellen, are you an animal lover? You know my cat, Zimba, and I think you like her. I'm going across the country to live with my daughter in California. She has two big dogs, and Zimba wouldn't survive there. She's an old kitty and just wants to stay warm and quiet."

Ellen gave a noncommittal reply, but went home later to think seriously about the cat. Zimba's life expectancy was probably not much more than her own. A cat doesn't have to be walked on a leash. With kitty litter and dry kibbles a cat could even stay alone overnight. Yet a warm, purring cat on your lap in the evening is a comforting thing.

Three weeks later, Janet had made her move to California and left her trailer with its darkened windows and screen door that slapped rhythmically in the wind. Ellen woke up each morning, her tired face still gray, that nagging cough continually present, and a sour taste in her mouth. Her hand, however, moved to Zimba's soft fur as the cat slept warmly on the blanket at the curve of Ellen's knee.

"Good company," she thought. "Just a cat, but she's good company." ❦

Now it's your turn. Make a list of various people you might consider as a protagonist for a story. Choose one person and brainstorm your character by making a table, like the following, and filling in the four columns. Then write a quick fifteen-minute draft and reread it using the guidelines given earlier. Remember to go easy on yourself. It's not easy to write fiction.

Dress, Body	Sayings, Foibles	Knows	Common Scenes

PART III

BRINGING TEACHER WRITING INTO THE CLASSROOM

You have been working on your own writing for some time now. You've tried the ten-minute quick writes and in rereading these pieces have discovered words, lines, and sections that mean a lot to you. You have taken some of these pieces and rewritten them. Most of all, you have felt your voice, the real you, emerging in your writing. It's time to step forward now and write something in front of your students or share with them a piece you have already written in the *My Quick Writes* notebook. It's time to bring your writing into your classroom.

Chances are you can't remember a teacher ever sharing her writing with you or even showing you her thinking while she was writing. Penny and I help you cross that threshold by showing you four teachers who, in the process of writing, demonstrate how it is done (see the accompanying DVD). Feel free to move between this book, the DVD, and the pieces you have already written in your *My Quick Writes* notebook in whatever way is most beneficial for you.

I know you are already asking, "With all that I have to do, and with time in ever shorter supply, why show what I'm writing to children?" There are five reasons why you should bring your writing into your classroom.

WATCH VICKI WRITE A MEMORY FROM SECOND GRADE WITH HER STUDENTS. (**CHOOSING A TOPIC:** "MODELING TOPIC CHOICE")

1. **WRITING WITH STUDENTS BUILDS RELATIONSHIPS AND NURTURES RESPECT AMONG ALL WRITERS IN THE ROOM.** Students feel connected to a teacher who writes about her feelings at the age her students are. A teacher's quick write on a conflict at recess when she was in school can help students process their own conflicts on the playground in healthy ways. Classrooms in which teachers and students write together are rich places where stories and life intersect and conferences occur writer to writer.

2. **WRITING WITH STUDENTS TEACHES THEM HOW TO SEE THINGS FROM A NEW POINT OF VIEW.** Imagine thirty sets of eyes all discovering something new. The joy of seeing what is different in each of us energizes writing classrooms. The power resides in you, the teacher, to nurture that creative energy in your classroom by showing through your writing how you see your life experiences.

LUCIE AND SUE ANN SHARE THEIR EXPERIENCES IN **CHOOSING A TOPIC:** "THE CLASSROOM ENVIRONMENT."

3. **WRITING TOGETHER CREATES ENERGY.** Students will take energy from your exploration of your writing, and they'll also begin to take energy from one another. So often the energy in teaching comes from discovering something that no one else has created. When you write with your students, you create something original every time you pick up your pen. Students will see your motivations as a writer and will want to create something new as well: your investment in writing will inspire a like investment on their part.

4. **MODELING YOUR DECISION-MAKING PROCESS HELPS THEM SEE THAT THE PROCESS IS ONGOING.** Your students already have many and varied models of *product:* terrific authors to read, poems and short stories you share, even the daily newspaper shows

students great writing. You are the model of the *process* writers go through to get there. You don't have to model exceptional writing; you model the decisions a writer makes: "I'm looking for the heartbeat here." "I like this word, it is more precise." "Oops, I've got to support this with a few details." You only need to write a little bit better than they do to be able to lead them to a new understanding about writing.

DON AND PENNY DISCUSS MODELING PROCESS IN THEIR **WRITER'S LIFE** INTERVIEW.

5. **WRITING WITH YOUR STUDENTS SAVES TIME.** Students who find topics they care about and who have been shown how to reread a text in order to refine it improve quickly as writers. The joy of revision replaces the ho-hum of completing assignments. A student listens with focused attention when the teacher uses a short story from her own life as a student to demonstrate a skill or strategy in writing.

I'm going to focus on five elements of teaching writing to start you on this journey: choosing a topic, rereading a text, using details, conferring, and using conventions. There are many more things to teach about writing, of course, and you should also deal with voice, organization, effective leads, all the other fine points you already understand about writing. I've simply chosen a few areas to get you started.

🌿

GETTING STARTED

Watch my interview with Vicki Hill at her home as she explains her concerns before she began writing with her students. Vicki starts at the easiest place there is, writing about something that happened to her when she was the students' age. Catch her as she shows her students her story about the goat that ate her paper. Yes, Vicki writes with her students, but what are they learning from her composing?

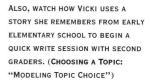

ALSO, WATCH HOW VICKI USES A STORY SHE REMEMBERS FROM EARLY ELEMENTARY SCHOOL TO BEGIN A QUICK WRITE SESSION WITH SECOND GRADERS. (**CHOOSING A TOPIC:** "**MODELING TOPIC CHOICE**")

There are three ways to share your writing. The first and easiest is to have written the piece beforehand. After you've read the piece aloud to your students, ask

1. What do they remember?

2. What stood out for them?

3. What are they wondering? (Take three or four questions.)

SUE ANN REREADS AN EDITORIAL SHE'S WRITTEN AND ASKS HER CLASS FOR FEEDBACK IN **REREADING A TEXT: "GUIDE, DON'T CORRECT."**

DEXTER ENTERTAINS TWO CHOICES FOR HIS DRAFT IN **CHOOSING A TOPIC: "QUICK WRITES."**

The next approach, which is a little more difficult, is to write your piece on a transparency ahead of time. Show the transparency while you read the text aloud and talk about the choices you entertained while writing.

The most difficult approach is to talk about your choices as you list them on the overhead, deciding what to do about those choices, and then write your piece on a transparency while the students watch.

I am often asked, "Won't the children be discouraged because their texts won't be as good?"

"Heavens, no," I reply, "the children are more fascinated by the subject than by the quality of the writing. They want to know about you, the teacher, and that is inside information. They want to know what you were doing and thinking when you were their age."

🌿

PRACTICE MAKES PERFECT

Once you have shared a few pieces of writing with your students, the progression from quick writes to rereading to finished drafts becomes easier. Penny Kittle talks about the process:

I wrote the first snapshot of "Basketball Dreams" while working with fifth graders. Their teacher read the short narrative "Flaws," from Linda Rief's marvelous book *100 Quickwrites,* and we all wrote for four minutes. What I heard in "Flaws" was a student's wish to be included, and I remembered my desire to play basketball. (I find that quick writes work best when the writer finds an unanticipated connection to the stimulus.)

When we moved to the second quick write (all drafts and notes are in Appendix D), I wrote more about basketball and added details that occurred to me as I reread. I was stretching out that moment as writers do. I liked the beginning, but I didn't work on the piece again for another month.

Then, when my seniors at the high school began experimenting with multigenre projects, I chose 1974—the year I turned thirteen— as my theme. The basketball story was a good fit. I used my quick write to sketch a draft. (The handwritten notes are the thoughts I had while rereading what I shared with my seniors.)

I sketched out four possible endings to the draft to model the choices I could make at that point in the story. Students always struggle with endings, so I modeled how to work through those decisions. The class discussion over which ending would be best was pretty heated, but no one wanted me to write the last one. I tried developing the first, then the second. I showed both versions to students, talking about how each one added to the original story and what readers might be thinking as they read it.

That day and for days to come I heard students mimicking the language I had used in my class conference: "You know, there's actually another way I could end this. I thought it should end with Grandma dying right there in the hospital, you know, but now I'm thinking I could write something else like about the funeral or the party or when we brought the headstone out to the cemetery."

My life stories provide me with opportunities to share writing decisions in class. Modeling the process balances all the polished writing my students read daily. My decisions are often copied by my students as they work through their own texts until they can make

SEE HOW TEACHERS HELP ELEMENTARY STUDENTS LEARN THE LANGUAGE OF WRITERS IN CONFERRING: "TEACHING YOUR STUDENTS TO SHARE."

those decisions on the basis of their own experiences in crafting writing.

⚬

CHOOSING A TOPIC

Anyone teaching writing has had to struggle with topic choice. The first year I taught writing, I assigned my students topics. I distinctly remember assigning the cue, Should There Be Capital Punishment? One of my students, who had a very open face, asked, "Does that mean we capitalize everything, Mr. Graves?"

"Of course not," I replied tartly, nipping his "joke" in the bud. His question had gone right over my head. Remembering this twenty years later, my face flushed with embarrassment: had David really thought everything should be capitalized? I'd given my seventh graders no background, little reading, yet I expected them to wax eloquently on a topic that meant little to them. In addition, most assigned writing is simply too long: students struggle for length instead of clarity. The implication is, "If it's long, it's good." We have to show them strong, short pieces of writing.

STUDENTS SHARE A WIDE RANGE OF TOPICS THEY WRITE ABOUT IN CHOOSING A TOPIC: "WHAT WRITING IS FOR."

My dissertation research showed that students initiated writing more often when topics were unassigned. I also reasoned that students had to know something about the subject and to have some passion for what they wrote about. But a stream of teachers kept lamenting, "I'm sick of violence; my students are choosing last night's sick TV plots. But you said to give them choice. What am I to do?"

I replied, "Accept the poor choice but take them on to better writing." Even I heard how lame that sounded: once children start off on a bad topic, it's hard to bring them into better writing. But I honestly didn't know what else to say.

Four years ago it struck me that we don't show students the source of our writing. We don't show them how we choose our topics.

We don't openly display the weighing of our choices. "Now this one is about the death of my dog, but I'm not ready for that just yet. This one is about a woodchuck that is raiding our garden. That one sounds promising. In fact, I'm angry at that woodchuck and here's why." I explain my anger. "This one is about fishing, but no, I think woodchuck is the one for me."

Think back to when you were weighing your choices for those first six quick writes I asked you to do in Part II. I suspect that several of them didn't turn out very well. It was difficult to be emotionally invested in the topic, or you just didn't know very much about the subject. That's par for the course on topic choice. Maybe you just weren't very good at choosing. You had to learn which territories served you better than others. *These* are the decisions we need to show students so that they can develop faith in their own process of making writing decisions. You can watch Sue Ann search her writing notebook for a topic for her writing on the DVD.

CHOOSING A TOPIC: "WRITE ABOUT WHAT YOU CARE ABOUT"

GETTING TO THE INSIDE OF A SUBJECT

You may have noticed that as you got used to doing quick writes you were able to get to the inside of some subjects right away. With others, you had to wrestle to find the center of what you wanted to write about. You'd get warmed up and by about the third paragraph you'd feel an emotional center. When you reread your text and put your finger on the heartbeat, you could see how to launch the subject more quickly. For the piece about my Uncle Nelson, I might have started with his addressing my friend Will, "Are you as dumb as [Donald] is?" to show that I just never knew what Uncle Nelson was going to say. I could then follow with the other details.

You need to demonstrate for the students the struggle to get to the center of a topic. Penny explains how she found the center of "Basketball Dreams" (see Appendix D):

When I began writing the quick write I just tried to capture that moment when I was sitting on the bench waiting to be chosen. I remembered how it felt, and I wanted to zoom in on the scene and show that to readers. In order to put readers in the scene, I tried to use a lot of physical detail. I wasn't sure if I was writing about Julia and me as friends or in relation to the boys I was so interested in or to explain why we were playing basketball on that team. Yet as I wrote those details and felt again how awful it all was, my anger at the teacher/coach and at myself rushed back. That quickly became the center for me; I could feel the emotion. It was only after I knew why I was writing the piece that I could consider endings that might work. When I brought the piece into my classroom, I took my students through that process in a ten-minute demonstration lesson.

Writers need to learn how to get to the emotional center quickly. They gain experience of the craft by doing a lot of quick writes followed by a rereading. They also start writing immediately on a bit of information that strikes them emotionally. Of course, the emotion has to be accompanied by details.

There is an added benefit here. Writing assessments are based on short prompts that allow little time for the student to get to the heart of the subject. Thus, when you show with your text how to get off the mark quickly, you provide a service that will be valuable throughout the rest of their education.

WRITING AT THE AGE OF YOUR STUDENTS

The easiest way to show students how to choose a topic is to write a short selection about an incident when you were their age. For example, if I were to write about an incident when I was in fourth grade I'd weigh my options about three incidents:

- How I got my nickname, Rabbit.
- Falling in love with Elisabeth.
- Building huts in the woods.

First, I have to *care* about each of these topics and incidents. My students have to know that I am emotionally involved. I say a little about each.

- "I had big ears and I was the smallest kid in the class. I got stuck with the nickname, Rabbit. I didn't like it at the time but I had no choice, the name was assigned to me, and I'd answer to it or not."

- "Right away I fell in love with Elisabeth, a lovely blond girl. Unfortunately, all the other boys were in love with her too."

- "I'd moved from the city to the country, and I had a dream of building a hut in the woods. I'd gotten a hatchet for my birthday and set out to use it by cutting birch saplings to make a lean-to."

Of course, I may care more about one topic than the other. In this case, I choose Elisabeth "because I'm curious about why I fell in love, my first love":

> When we moved to East Greenwich, Rhode Island, I felt like a stranger in my own classroom with Ms. McGraw. Our teacher had a loud voice and I could feel a heavy feeling in my stomach. In the midst of feeling lonely, I quickly focused on Elisabeth. She had long blond hair, lovely blue eyes, a deep voice. She was a second soprano so that when we changed our seats for music I sat right behind her. I simply couldn't keep my eyes off her. Of course, I didn't take in the fact that none of the other boys could keep their eyes off her either.

You may be unable to remember an incident that took place when you were the exact age your students are. That's okay. Choose an incident when you were a little older (or a little younger). The important thing is for children to understand that

1. The point of writing is to communicate with oneself and with others.

2. Writers feel strongly about something and use language to convey that feeling.

3. Those feelings give rise to essential details that reflect the feeling.

REREADING A TEXT

I teach children to reread their work because it saves me so much time when *I* read their work. I want to see indications on the page that reveal their rereading. At the very least I want to see the heartbeat sentence underlined. Of course, learning to reread is a lifetime proposition. I am still trying hard to learn how to reread my own work. A writer spends 95 percent of his time alone with words on paper; why shouldn't he learn to reread?

Children don't like to reread their writing any more than adults do. I see second graders calculating how many sentences they need to reach the end of the page and hear their sighs of satisfaction once the last line is written. The more conscientious students check their spelling, grammar, and punctuation. Then they immediately turn to new work and move on.

Sometimes when I write, I make changes as I go along on my computer, but I secretly know I should do that much later in the process. My first rereading should be to read the piece aloud and to indicate those words and phrases that I like. Traditionally, most writers are taught to first look for what they did wrong, making the first rereading a negative experience.

Think back to the exercises when you searched first for good words and lines that satisfied you. Your next task was to find the line that contained the heartbeat, the *you* in the piece, your wish for the piece. This was more difficult. I want children to appreciate their first words and to feel the possibilities in their lines. Children need to be shown how to do this, not told, and shown not once but every time we write.

LUCIE REREADS HER STORY AS A DEMONSTRATION FOR HER SECOND GRADERS IN **REREADING A TEXT:** "A WRITER'S RESPONSIBILITY."

WHAT DO I LIKE?

Take a quick-write prompt, read it aloud, show how you uncover the topics suggested in it, make your process of choosing one visible, and then write on that topic. I'll do it with you. My prompt follows.

> The other day I heard a cat crying in an alley. Well, I think he was crying. He sure was making a loud noise. I don't have a pet and it hit me that maybe I could take the cat home and tell my Mom he was lost and had nowhere to go.

Here are three topics that I'm thinking about.

1. First, I can't stand to hear a cat or any animal crying.

2. We had a cat named Tommy when I was growing up and I remember when he burned his paws.

3. I remember finding a cat once and when I asked Mother if we could keep him she said, "You'd better check his collar to see if he has one and then I need to think about it."

Tommy's burning his paws was pretty scary; I think I'll write about that.

> Our cat Tommy was curious about everything. That's the way cats are. We had one of those stoves where there's a big door that you pull down for the oven. Mother had just baked a pie in the oven and she left the door open. It was still hot from

> baking the pie. Tommy leaped up on top of the oven, peered down into it, then jumped down on to the open oven door. Poor Tommy let out a yowl as his paws hit the hot door, went straight up in the air, down to the floor. I raced after him, and the last picture I have of him is holding one paw in the air at the bottom of the cellar stairs and waving it as if to say, "My paws are killing me."

What are some words that I like? I like *curious, peered, yowl,* and *waving.* Is there a sentence or a phrase that I like? No question, it's the last one: "I raced after him, and the last picture I have of him is holding one paw in the air at the bottom of the cellar stairs and waving it as if to say, 'My paws are killing me.'" The sentence just keeps going. I can see Tommy at the bottom of the stairs.

It depends on the age of your students, but asking them to share just the words and sentences they like most is probably enough. I recommend that children do three or four quick writes (but not all on the same day!) just appreciating words and sentences. Of course, some of them may not find anything they appreciate, either because they've read a lot of good stories or because they're struggling learners. Ask the good readers to put in some more precise words. Ask the struggling learners to read a sentence to the class and let their classmates identify a few words they liked and say why.

WHAT SENTENCE IS ME? WHAT IS MY WISH FOR THE PIECE?

Here's another example. I'm asked to write to this prompt: "You like to let snakes twine up your arm. You love the feel of those scales working their way up." I think about three possibilities.

1. I made my dad nervous when I let a snake crawl up my arm. Dad didn't like snakes.

2. We got a cobra last year that was in a bottle. The hood on the cobra gave me the willies.

3. When I mow the lawn and I see a snake I mow right over it. I suppose I shouldn't do that.

I think I will write about the first possibility. It was an experience that actually happened to me.

> I used to watch garter snakes twine in and out of the rocks when I was a kid. It was hot in summer so they liked to get into the crevices. One day I picked one up just behind the head just to see what it felt like. They weren't greasy or slimy. I let the snake go up my arm. One day my dad came outside and saw me doing that.
>
> I could tell he was upset, and he said they could bite me if I didn't watch out. I said they wouldn't, but when I was talking to him and looking at him, the snake did bite me. Dad said, "I told you he would." I said, "It didn't hurt one bit," even though I had two tiny punch holes in my little finger.

This time when I reread I need to find a sentence that sounds most like me. Where do I find emotion in the piece that shows my personality? I was a pretty stubborn kid so it is probably the sentence, "'It didn't hurt one bit,' even though I had two tiny punch holes in my little finger." Do you have an opinion about which one shows me the most?

Now I have to think of the wish I had for this piece. I guess I'd wish that people could see that I liked snakes but my dad didn't, and it got me into a little trouble. Do I have a wish line? I think this is it: "One day my dad came outside and saw me doing that. I could tell he was upset, and he said they could bite me if I didn't watch out. I said they wouldn't, but when I was talking to him and looking at him, the snake did bite me." I think this sentence shows how I was different from Dad in my regard for snakes. Do you think there's another place that shows my wish?

WHERE IS THE HEARTBEAT?

I now read prompt number 2 under Getting Started in the *My Quick Writes* notebook: "One time I was with my horse. . . ." I consider three options for a quick write.

1. I remember watching wild west movies and wishing I had a horse to ride.

2. My parents had so many questions: where would you keep it? How would you pay for the feed?

3. Maybe my parents would talk to me about how much I'd want a horse. They'd try to hear me out with no promises.

I'd really like it if my parents would try to understand why I wanted a horse, so I think I'll write about that.

> I'd just come in from a Saturday afternoon movie and I dreamed of the day I'd sit high on a horse. The other kids would think me big up on that horse. The girl I liked would think me big.
>
> But my parents said, "So you want a horse. How come you want a horse all of a sudden?"
>
> I said, "I want to be able to ride a horse."
>
> "Well, if all you want is to ride one, I guess we could see about that."
>
> "No, I want to own one, have one for myself. I'd take care of it."
>
> "Where would you keep the horse? How would you feed it and pay for it?"
>
> I didn't know what to say. Tears came to my eyes. I said, "I just want one. You figure it out."

The heartbeat isn't the same as the wish, but it's very similar. I ask myself, "Where am I really revealed here?" My real reason for wanting a horse may be just to have one. My guess is the heartbeat is in the sentence, "No, I want to own one, have one for myself." Do you think I am accurate? The heartbeat contains feeling, but it also shows the main idea of the piece. The two go together.

Children usually need help with this important step. They are gauging their feelings and looking for where they appear in the text. They are looking for the emotional, detailed center. Sometimes this is much easier to do with a partner. The writer can read the piece aloud and the partner can listen for the heartbeat. For children who don't enter into a piece, who keep writing at a distance, this step can be very difficult. Finding the heartbeat is a lifelong pursuit. The more complex the piece, the more difficult it is to find the emotional center.

WATCH DEXTER FIND THE HEARTBEAT IN HIS QUICK WRITES. (USING DETAILS: "FINDING YOUR VOICE")

WHAT MAY NOT BELONG?

Deletion begins with the lines that are farthest off from the emotional center. Even though every sentence may seem to belong in a piece, it is useful to check to see which writing is farthest off from the lines containing the heartbeat. Although they are first cousins of the heartbeat, the two lines I choose are: "The other kids would think me big up on that horse. The girl I liked would think me big." These lines will probably stay in the piece, but it is always a good exercise to perform.

WHAT HAPPENS IF I MOVE THE HEARTBEAT?

Sometimes it is interesting to experiment with a piece by moving the heartbeat up to the first line. This allows us and our students to get used to "just saying it." (This technique is especially useful when writing to a prompt on a test.) I'll move the heartbeat line and see what happens:

> "No, I want to own one, have one for myself," I fired back, when my parents said I could easily find a horse to ride in our area. What I really wanted was my own horse to feed, to take care of, and especially to ride around and show off. I wanted the other kids to see me riding high on my own horse.

See how quickly I get off the mark and cut away much of the other writing I put in the first draft. Moving the heartbeat to the first line doesn't always work, but it is worth considering. Some of your students may be ready to try it. The challenge is to know how to fill in the necessary background for the reader.

HAVE I FOLLOWED THE NATURAL ORDER?

Read aloud prompt number 6 under Quick Writes for Children in the *My Quick Writes* notebook.

> My coach is cool. . . . Write about the kind of coach you have.

First, I need to think of the possibilities for this piece. Have a group of ten children share their individual takes on the prompt. Here are three of mine.

1. Before Little League everyone played. We just said, "Let's go out and play."

2. Right field is where they put the players who aren't very good fielders. I used to pray that no balls would come my way.

3. Some coaches are just about winning, and all the kids don't play.

I feel very strongly about coaches who don't let everyone play, so I think I'll write about number three.

> We got a paper at home in the spring that said if we went out for the team, we'd get to play. They said it was about partici-pation. I'm a pitcher and a right fielder. I know I'm not so good, and the only time I get in is when we're ahead by about fifteen runs. I don't get to pitch, so the coach puts me out in right field. So twice I've gotten into games so far this year.
>
> Even when we practice, I don't get in. Our coach is only about winning. You should hear him during the game. He yells at the kids, the umps, even the kids on the other team. Base-ball used to be fun, but it isn't fun any more.

Before I can check the natural order of things, I need to find the heartbeat of the piece. The heartbeat seems to be: "I know I'm not so good, and the only time I get in is when we're ahead by fifteen runs." Natural order refers to the chronology, one thing happening logically after the other. The natural order in this piece begins in the spring, when we're told that everyone can play. I make the counterpoint that I don't get to play and give some examples. My conclusion: "Our coach is only about winning." My subtler point, only slightly related to the heartbeat, is that the coach yells about everything. He doesn't seem to be enjoying himself, and therefore I'm not either.

HOW EFFECTIVE ARE MY VERBS AND NOUNS?

Writers write principally with verbs and nouns. Stuff (nouns) needs to move (verbs) gracefully and economically. Although adjectives re-ferring to nouns and adverbs referring to verbs are sometimes neces-sary, good writers try to stay away from them. This kind of work is more advanced. By the end of the year, though, some of your better writers may be ready to examine nouns and verbs more closely. Here's another prompt for a quick write.

> I miss my grandma. She's so much fun when she's here, but she lives so far away. She only comes once a year. What happened was we moved away from her, because my dad had to take a new job. My grandma and I used to talk a lot but not any more.

Here are three different approaches I might take.

1. I have two grandmas. One is full of fun and adventure. The other one is so serious, works hard, and doesn't laugh much.

2. One of our great adventures is driving to Grandma's house. It's about two hundred miles away. When we finally arrive, we charge out of the car and run inside. She wants to know everything about each one of us.

3. One year we tried to drive to Grandma's house and a snowstorm came up and we had to turn around. We were all crying and so sad.

Even though all of these are real, I think I'll take number three; that was a sad, sad day.

> Seven of us piled into our station wagon for the trip to Grandma's house. This was a long trip to take and we had games, toys, food for every fifty miles. We were all in a good mood, but suddenly we could see dark on the horizon. The dark turned into a snowstorm. We kept going for about a half hour until we'd slowed down to thirty miles an hour. It was very slippery too. Dad finally said, "I'm sorry kids, but we've got to go back home." We couldn't believe it. Some of us started to cry.

> We kept saying, "We want to go to Grandma's house."
> We took the toys and food and started to play again, but we
> were going back the other way. We called Grandma when we
> got back to the house. It was a very sad call.

I begin by looking at the first five nouns: *station wagon, trip, house, trip,* and *games.* These are good nouns, and I sense a lot of information behind each one. Now I check the first five verbs: *piled, was, take, had,* and *were.* The first one creates an image, but the others are auxiliary verbs that need to be more precise in order to get the nouns in motion. The poor nouns are waiting for better verbs that will make the trip more exciting! Here is a rewrite to make the text more active.

> We knew this journey lasted about ten hours, so we grabbed a
> box from the barn and loaded in toys, games, and other doo-
> dads for every fifty miles.

🦢

USING DETAILS

Young writers' pieces are continually marked down when they write to prompts on writing assessments because they don't supply enough detail. One of the problems is the prompt doesn't elicit significant details. Still, with enough practice on quick writes, writers should be experienced enough to supply the necessary details.

Claims usually come in the form of declarative sentences such as,

- He hated the Yankees.
- She bought a beautiful dress.
- You wouldn't believe the size of the fish he caught.
- It isn't fair that we have to take tests.

- The fifth grade is taking over the playground.

- The food in our cafeteria doesn't taste very good.

Statements like these cry out for either a story or a tight essay. Above all, they require details. Ask your students to find declarative sentences or claims. Have them number (1, 2, 3, etc.) the details that support the claim.

Dexter demonstrates how to add details that are important to the moment in Using Details: "Finding Your Voice."

Why is it so difficult for both children and adults to supply evidence for their readers? Lev Vygotsky (1962) talks about a child making his first attempt to write. The child sees his dog and wants to write about the dog. Let's say the child draws the dog sitting under a tree next to some flowers. The dog in the picture is of course much larger than the tree or flowers, because the dog is more important. The entire scene is in the child's head, but when he goes to write about it, he abstracts it as, "I see the dog." The child then picks up his pencil and laboriously sounds out the letters and possibly runs them together: *Icedadg*. But the entire scene is still present in those letters, and the child will look back and forth between the text and his drawing, talking about what he sees. It's like a conversation: each person supplies language in response to the other. If the details aren't there, someone asks, "So what was she wearing? Then what did they do?"

But when a writer writes, she is utterly alone. She must anticipate the reader's questions and answer them. Even more important, the writer must care about her reader.

Second grader Robbie writes about when he won a ribbon for his pigs at the Grange fair. The teacher asks how he won the ribbon. Robbie explains it was because his sow had so many piglets. The teacher nudges, "That's very interesting Robbie; don't you think you ought to put that in this piece?"

"If the kids want to know I'll tell them," he replies.

"But do you remember when you were absent last Thursday and Friday? What would the kids do then?" It has never occurred to

Robbie that he won't always be there to answer questions as in oral discourse. Writing is that unique medium in which the author doesn't need to be present for his audience to understand what he means.

The child must move beyond thinking only of self, must care about the audience. This is an enormous leap in development, moving beyond the rigors of getting something down on the page to considering the people who will read it. This usually means observing the conventions that allow a reader to say, "Oh, so this is about catching the big fish?"

Not until the writer has had experience with many audiences, including her teacher, the other children in the class, and her parents, will she realize the need for further details. Too often, attention is paid first to etiquette (conventions) before ideas, the telling of a story, the heartbeat. Even worse, in some classrooms the child may have but one audience: the teacher. In that case, the child may just want to complete the assignment and be done with it. It is better to get students writing for real audiences and anticipating their questions.

SUE ANN TEACHERS STUDENTS ABOUT THE AUDIENCE FOR A STANDARDIZED ASSESSMENT IN **USING DETAILS**: "FINDING YOUR VOICE."

FIND THE CLAIMS THAT REQUIRE DETAILS

When I write "My wife is curious," the word *curious* cries for details. The line hangs in the air waiting to be propped up by supporting evidence, by details. My problem is that I assume that everyone has the same access to Betty's curiosity. It is all very clear to me that she is curious. Unfortunately, other people don't know what I know. Having made the claim "My wife is curious," I must supply the details to back it up. I write:

Betty will stop dead on a trail, studying scat. "Now is this fox, dog, or coyote?" She studies the width, length, and color of the scat.

She examines more closely to catch a clue about what the animal has been eating. Another ten paces she'll notice a pink moth on a wildflower. ❧

In my poem about being in first grade I make the claim that "everything is edible." Even though it is a poem, I must provide the evidence to make my point.

> In first grade
> Everything is edible,
> Soft, primary pencil wood
> To run my teeth down
> Like corn on the cob.

VICKI ENCOURAGES HER SECOND GRADERS TO HELP HER ADD DETAILS TO HER WRITING PIECE IN **USING DETAILS: "FINDING THE DETAILS."**

What follows are four quick-write paragraphs. Find the claims, the declarative sentences that require details, and then write those details. I'll help you with the first one.

> We're supposed to go on a vacation. I hate getting ready. My Dad is upset, my Mom isn't ready, my sister's taking care of the cat, and the cat has to come with us. My pack's all set so what's the matter with the other guys?

1. **"WE'RE SUPPOSED TO GO ON A VACATION."** Where are the details that show where you are supposed to be going? "We're supposed to go to Mt. Desert Island, and it's three hundred miles away. Vacations aren't fun until you get there."

2. **"MY DAD IS UPSET."** Where are the details that show that Dad is upset? "Dad keeps saying, 'There isn't room enough. How will we ever get it all in?' He keeps pacing back and forth out by the tailgate."

3. **"MY MOM ISN'T READY."** Where are the details that show that Mom isn't ready? "Mom's suitcase is still open. The telephone

rang, and she's been talking to Aunt Lucy for twenty minutes. The food box is only half full."

Here are the remaining three paragraphs.

> I ride the city bus and it takes me two transfers to get there. My dad says, "You go to a good school and I don't care how long it takes you to get there." But when it snows the bus takes so long it makes me late. The principal looks at me funny when I come in. I say, "I couldn't help it." I wish I didn't have so far to go.

> Mr. Gibbons stands down by the garbage when we dump our trays. He stares at me like he's trying to make me feel guilty. Hey, if they cook horrible food, why shouldn't I dump it? After all, I paid for it. What does he care?

> How do you survive without a best friend? Timmy and I have known each other since first grade. He lives just down the street from me and our parents know each other. We watch the same TV and we're Red Sox fans. He likes Manny and I like Ortiz. We even read the same books. Tell me about your best friend.

A FINAL MISUNDERSTANDING ABOUT ADDING DETAIL

In a classroom Penny Kittle was observing, a teacher was trying to elicit more detail in a child's piece. The child has written: "On vacation we went to Disney World. We went on Space Mountain." When his teacher told him he needed to add more detail, the child wrote:

> We took a car to the hotel and then went to Disney World. We paid for our tickets and then we went in. We rode on Space

Mountain first. Then we had lunch. I had a pizza. Then we rode on Space Mountain again. 🌾

Here was a clear case of adding more declarative, boring sentences just to lengthen the story. In the child's mind, "It is better if it is longer." Penny told the boy to focus on one noun in the narrative, put it on another page, and write about only it. She stopped the narrative flow and helped him to choose one scene on which to focus. This is a very important step. Until this moment comes, "more detail" may mean more writing that doesn't improve the piece.

🌾

CONFERRING: BEING AN AUDIENCE

I have been conducting conferences for nearly twenty-five years, and each year I gain new insights. Every year I ask myself, what are conferences for? My latest answer is, conferences help the writer maintain skillful control of the piece. The writer has a wish for the piece, and I want to help her accomplish that wish with a sense of satisfaction. Nevertheless, some pieces should be abandoned with dignity. The writer simply made a bad choice or must put off writing about this topic until she knows more about it. Perhaps the writer has for whatever reason lost touch with the pulse of what she is saying.

As students learn how to reread their work, I expect them to have gone back to a piece on their own before I have a conference with them. Of course, I can't ask them to do a first rereading unless I have taught them how to do this with my own text.

Effective writing instruction includes many opportunities for conferences. (Examples of many types of conferences are included on the DVD.) Types of conferences include:

1. Teacher-to-student

2. Student-to-teacher

LUCIE WRESTLES FOR CONTROL OF HER WRITING WITH HER EAGER-TO-HELP SECOND GRADERS IN REREADING A TEXT: "A WRITER'S RESPONSIBILITY."

TYPES OF CONFERENCES SHOWN ON THE DVD INCLUDE ONE-ON-ONE, SMALL-GROUP, AND FISHBOWL. (CONFERRING)

3. Student-to-student

4. Author's chair

5. Chosen audience

6. Colleague-to-colleague

CONFERRING: "TEACHING YOURSELF TO SHARE"

TEACHER-TO-STUDENT CONFERENCES

To demonstrate a teacher-to-student conference, I ask one of my stronger students to be ready to tell me words and phrases he likes, where the heartbeat of his piece is, and what information supports that heartbeat. For the demonstration, I simply ask the student to read a portion of the piece. Here's an example:

> I have two dogs. One is a border collie, and the other is an Australian sheep dog. The collie is small but the sheep dog is really big.
>
> When I go for a hike the two dogs are always with me. You should see them play with each other. They chase each other up the trail and back again. They nip at each other and spin around and around when they are playing.
>
> Some people think they are fighting, but I know they are only playing. Every once in a while they stop and look to see where I am. ⚹

I then ask, "Tell me about your piece." I expect the student to provide the details itemized above, like this:

> I have these two dogs. I like the part where I say, "They nip at each other and spin around." That's good action. For the heartbeat I'm not so sure. But I show the action in the nipping and spinning and when I say, just before that, "They chase each other up the trail and back again." I wanted to show my dogs in action, so maybe that's where the heartbeat is." ⚹

I then ask the class to respond to what the student has said. "That's good detail. What do you think, class?"

"That last sentence is pretty good because it shows the connection between you and the dogs: 'Every once in a while they stop and look to see where I am.' There's feeling in that," responds one student.

It may be that as writers we decide the heartbeat is in a different location. It is up to us, however, to say why it is elsewhere. I cannot stress how difficult it is to locate the heartbeat in a text. First, the student has to care about the piece and have expended some emotion in creating it. Second, the student has to step back and locate the nexus of those feelings. Third, the student has to look at the details contained at that nexus.

WATCH DEXTER SHOW HIS CLASS HOW TO FIND THE HEARTBEAT IN REREADING A TEXT: "FIND THE PULSE."

STUDENT-TO-TEACHER CONFERENCES

SEE SUE ANN AND A STUDENT CONFER IN FRONT OF THE CLASS. (CONFERRING: "SUE ANN'S FISHBOWL CONFERENCE")

Once I'm sure that a few students know how to start rereading their own texts, I ask two of them to volunteer to confer with me in front of the class about something I've written. (I project a transparency of the piece so everyone can follow along.) Here's the text.

I like to do cross-country skiing. But I don't really like it until I get out there. There's so much preparation: the right wax, heavy layers for warmth, mittens, hat. Then I load it into the car. I'm wearing my trail pass. I can't forget that.

Finally, I'm on the trail. I do some warm-ups and finally stretch out. After about ten minutes I'm into the rhythm and my body just feels good reaching, driving the poles, and feeling the swoosh of the snow under my skis. It is a little cold at first but the scenery of snow-covered hemlocks adds a special touch to the near-silent glide through the trees.

I read the piece aloud and wait for the students to begin.

Andrew asks, "What are some phrases or words that you like?

"I don't really care for this piece until I get to the actual skiing. I like parts of the last two sentences: 'my body just feels good reaching, driving the poles, and feeling the swoosh of the snow under my skis' and 'snow-covered hemlocks adds a special touch to the near-silent glide through the trees.'"

Clinton asks, "And what about the heartbeat?"

"Strange, but those two sentences contain the heartbeat for this very short cross-country skiing piece. Now I am skiing and I like the silence that goes with the effort of going down the trail."

Andrew and Clinton turn to the class. "Where do you think the heartbeat is located?"

Someone volunteers, "I think the sentence that begins, 'After about ten minutes I'm into the rhythm,' starts the heartbeat section.

"Yes, it probably does," I say. Now my job as a writer is to explore the heart of the story. I've uncovered the heartbeat, so I prop it up with details that expand it.

STUDENT-TO-STUDENT CONFERENCES

When I think students have internalized the basic facets of a conference, I ask them to find a partner, sit side by side, and go to work. I deliberately limit the time that they are to stay on task: five minutes for a quick write, three minutes for rereading, and four minutes for the conference. Then I have a group share in which partners report on how their conferences went.

WATCH STUDENTS CONFER WITH PARTNERS. (CONFERRING: "TEACHING YOUR STUDENTS TO SHARE")

AUTHOR'S-CHAIR CONFERENCES

The author's chair has been around since the early 1980s. I first encountered one in Ellen Blackburn Karelitz's New Hampshire classroom, where child authors sat in a special chair to read their pieces aloud or to read aloud from a book that was important to them. Since that time, the author's chair has evolved in many directions. The point of the author's-chair conference is for an audience of peers to listen attentively and share a range of opinions.

Here's how it works. A child reads his piece aloud, then says, "Comments, questions, and reminders?" His classmates make comments, ask questions, and share what the piece reminds them of, what memories have been triggered. Children often raise many questions. You need to observe these conferences very carefully: too many questions and reminders can cause the author in the chair to lose control of the piece and of the conference. Also, the reading should never take more than three minutes. If a piece is longer than this, the author should read a portion of the text, after first providing some background about where it fits within the entire piece.

In the following example, a child shares a portion of a quick write.

> Our family took a trip to New York City. We went by car. The car is new and I think that's why my dad wanted to take a trip with the family. It cost my dad a fortune to park the car. He forgot how much parking costs in New York City. We walked in Central Park. I loved seeing the horses prancing along the paths. I'd never been that close to horses before. Then we went to the Empire State Building, and took the ferry out to Ellis Island. ✣

Then he asks his classmates, "What do you remember?"

"You took a trip to New York."

"I remember your dad's car."

"I remember the horses."

"Parking was expensive."

"You took the ferry to Ellis Island."

I ask the author, "What did we forget?"

The author says, "You didn't remember we went to the Empire State Building." Then he asks, "What struck you? Where do you think the heartbeat is in this piece?"

"I think you liked being near the horses. I liked that part, too."

"I think you liked being in the new car."

The author zeroes in: "Where do you think the heartbeat is in this piece?"

"I think it is where you were in the park with the horses."

"You said you'd never been that close to horses before. I wish you'd say more about the horses. Were they really big?"

"They were huge. They were sleek and shiny."

"Do you think the horse part is where the heartbeat is?"

"I suppose so."

"You should put in the details you just told us."

This is genuine audience reaction. My role is to keep the process on track, help the author and audience play their respective roles. If the author hasn't shown where he is involved in the piece, I ask, "Tell us about the place in the piece that means most to you." Personal involvement is what I'm looking for.

In this case, I go back to the nouns in the piece: *car, park, horses, Empire State Building, Ellis Island,* and *ferry.* I want to know what information stands behind those nouns. I say to the child, "I'm going to say some words to you from your piece. Tell me which one means the most to you." I want the child to step out of the onrushing narrative and make a selection. Or I may turn to the class and say, "Ask her questions about horses."

CHOSEN-AUDIENCE CONFERENCES

Sometimes a student is afraid to read to the entire class and needs a more limited audience. I ask the child to select two or three other children—usually a very safe audience of friends—to hear their short piece. The format follows as if it were a larger group: the author reads the piece to the group, and the audience cites the components, tells what struck them, and discusses the heartbeat. Comments and questions follow.

COLLEAGUE-TO-COLLEAGUE CONFERENCES

CONFERRING: "TEACHING YOURSELF TO SHARE"

Teachers can learn to confer about writing by talking with colleagues. One way to develop your own writing is by working with other teachers in a writing group. On the DVD you can observe three writing groups at work: Sue Ann meets with one colleague for a writing lunch; Dexter and two colleagues process their writing after school; and Lucie, Vicki, Ramie (the class paraprofessional), and Don meet to talk about writing. Eavesdrop on these conversations. Find a colleague, grab a cup of dark roast coffee, a bag of chocolates, and begin exploring writing. It's a recipe for magic.

In the following section, Penny Kittle tells about her writing group at Kennett High School, in Conway, New Hampshire.

✺

WRITING WITH TEACHERS

As writers we are always exploring what happens, what comes next, turning it over, finding words to sit in like chairs . . . because words shape the strange sorrows we are living in, help us connect.

—Naomi Shihab Nye

Eben started it.

He sent out a note about beginning a writing group for teachers. Problem was, no one could read it; Eben has the worst handwriting of anyone I know. Enough of us asked him to explain, I guess, because at our first meeting there were four English teachers, pens and notebooks ready. He chose this god-awful time of 6:30 on Friday mornings, but we went anyway.

I was curious. Eben had that writer look about him: shaggy brown hair and pleated khakis, looked like he lived on coffee and cigarettes, packed away in a small apartment building. I had been on the hiring committee and knew Eben had done graduate work at the University of New Hampshire. The name alone made me shudder—the Mt. Rushmore of writing, with Don Graves, Don Murray, Tom Newkirk, and Jane Hansen carved across a gray granite shelf. Eben could undoubtedly teach me something.

I loved writing; in fact, I had dreamed of being an author as a child. I just never had time for it, never wrote anything except checks and sporadically in a private journal I've kept since college. I listened when Nancie Atwell said teachers should learn to write themselves in order to teach students how to write. Problem was, almost all writing teachers I knew were too busy deciphering student drafts and editing them, reading short stories and novels to use in class, and never writing anything themselves except notes to parents and students. It's a harried life, believe me. Who has time to love and nurture what we teach? I thought I was ahead of the rest because I wrote journal entries with my students. I rarely crafted a piece beyond a clean rough draft, though, and therein lies all the difference. I knew I had been waiting for this moment. It was a next step for me. It was time to become a writer.

We gathered in our cramped department office, sitting in orange, stackable chairs, the brown stain of a ceiling leak snaking down one wall. It was winter and out the window behind us the morning light played with the silvery sheen of ice. Eben gave us a topic: morning. We wrote and wrote and then we stopped and shared. Eben's piece was a ride. I was in the car with him, wandering along the highway. I could feel the curves in the road. It was only ten or fifteen lines, but I could see it when we crested the next hill. I didn't want to share after that; I just wanted to write like him.

It was awkward to regurgitate my writing, on the spot, when I knew it wasn't much. I wasn't alone. My colleagues shifted nervously in their chairs. There was an awkward silence whenever one of us finished reading. Eben noticed and said we should all bring something we were working on to our next meeting. A deadline would force us to write, he reasoned, and then we could give one another feedback. Now there's terror for you; I had to bring something I prepared ahead of time. I couldn't hide behind *I only had ten minutes to write and it's early and I'm tired.* I had to craft something and copy it for people.

Suddenly I had nothing to write about. I sweated over a story. Hours later it was still lurching along, with stilted transitions and little vision. I could feel a spot of panic in my stomach, reminding me that I called myself a writing teacher but couldn't write. I knew I could miss the next few writers-group meetings and go on hiding. No one would call me on it. They would all believe I was just too busy; they're teachers after all. No one said I had to write, except me. But every once in awhile one sentence would come out well, maybe two or three strung together. I could hear my voice, and I liked the sound of the words I put together. It wasn't much, but it was a start.

We met in Eben's room in the basement of the school a week later, below exposed pipes painted a hideous yellow-green. Again there were four of us: we had lost one of our original number, but the principal showed up instead. Go figure. I had invited her, but I couldn't believe she came, a piece of writing in one hand, her beeper in the other. She was paged twice on the intercom while she tried to share her piece. She finally gave up. She never returned to our group, and I can't say I was sorry. I didn't need my boss there beside me as I learned something I was sure I should know already. I made sure everyone else shared before me that morning so that we ran out of time for mine, but I learned a few things and took those lessons with me when I approached my piece again.

That first year we probably met six times in all. It was scarier than teaching. The best part was watching Eben's students arriving for class watching us as we continued talking about the piece before us. I thought it was important that those students saw teachers haggling over leads, playing with structure and voice, quibbling over the impact individual words had. I had never seen anyone process writing like that in all of my years of schooling.

The following year we gelled as a team and began weekly meetings in my classroom: Eben, Ed, Carrie, and I. We laughed until we cried. We surprised one another, we listened to and counseled one another, and tore apart our writing with confidence. Eben and Ed wrote poetry. I stuck with narratives, but I watched their moves carefully. I learned what was important in a poem, and it changed how I teach poetry. If Carrie dropped a piece in my box on Monday it was like a personal challenge: was I still writing? And I'd think, damn, I wish I could write like her. I'd carve out the time to write that night and discover energy for teaching my classes the following day. My pieces coached me in the moves writers make, and I was eager to share these lessons with my students.

My colleagues' criticism stung. I didn't like it. You have to be careful when you're correcting someone's work. I don't think I'd ever been careful enough with my students. It was so easy to just tell them what wasn't working and think that was helping. In writers group I learned quickly that compliments showed me what I could do and gave me confidence, criticism confirmed my fears and left me frustrated. When I confidently approached a piece to revise it, I was playful. When I went back to one in frustration, I usually made it worse. One of my favorite readers asks questions when he's confused by my writing. He doesn't point out weak leads, broken paragraphs, rabbit trails. He asks. I never feel inadequate with him. That's the teacher I want to be for my students.

We need to nurture the fire that made us English teachers. We should contribute pieces to the school literary magazine or perform at the next poetry slam. We must process writing with our students, not stand apart from them as the authority when we are afraid to try the craft ourselves. We should give our colleagues the gift of having written and give our students the gift of having a writer for a teacher. We have to find the time. Poetry and short stories won't come easy for any of us, but we need an inside view of what we are asking of our students. I'm launching a research project this week in class, and I will do research as well. I'm going to gather facts on note cards and struggle to tie the ideas together. I'd rather not, but how will I teach this well if I don't?

Ed shared a piece in January that reminds me of why it is worth the effort. He brought it still warm from the copy machine; he'd written the draft just minutes before. It was a fishing story, but a life story as well. Ed took a student out to a lake last spring, a foreign exchange student just days from heading home. They fished together and watched a rainbow dance across the water. Two days later the boy drowned. Ed's piece made us all cry. I hadn't known Ed grieved for this lost boy, half a world from his home. I didn't know a repeated phrase in his poem would imitate my heartbeat, my blood pumping through my veins. I felt the power of poetry draw us together that afternoon, as clouds covered the sun and our room became cool and dark. It is why writing matters, why we must teach our students to do it well. Our lives, and theirs, are filled with such stories waiting to be told.

🐾

FIVE YEARS LATER:
THE GROUP REMAINS

I write to hold what I find in my life in my hands and to declare it a treasure.

—Lucy Calkins

I sit at my desk on a Sunday, late afternoon light coming in through the windows, and leaf through three file folders of stories. I've saved them for years. The handwriting in the margins is all familiar now—Ed's determined script; Eben's half-formed mystical scribbles; Carrie's precise and elegant print; Ryan's fat little letters next to an arrow pointing toward a place in the writing that moved him.

Fab title. I snicker. Thanks for noticing, Ryan.

I want some of your dialogue here. You're almost too smooth. You're right. I can do that. I'm glad you thought of it, Eben.

Penny, I admire your courage and convictions. There are days when I don't know where to stuff my frustrations. This reminds me to write! If you have any doubts, you rock! I love this guy. He stood at my door once with a piece I'd written in his hand. He said, "Kittle, this latest piece. Wooooh. Go, dog, go."

You force me to pause, to think, to feel the oh-so-human angst of youth, frailty, and parenthood. Ed always sees deeply and helps me to see more.

A writing group is about more than writing. There is a deep connection with these people forged from stories of pain and loss, laughter and longing, hopes and even our deepest fears. We share. We are heard. We write together and try to make sense of living. I could tell you it's simpler than that, make it sound tidy and professional, but it isn't; it's our lives in all their messy complexity.

Ed reminded me last week that each day as a teacher we have to prioritize: "I'll do this; I'll let that go. And then I'll have to live with myself for letting it go." We teachers think carefully about how to apportion time, so I'm sure you're wondering how a writing group can be the best place to spend some of yours.

It's all about energy.

It starts with my first thoughts about a piece of writing: the energy to create. I feel the power of the blank page. Anything goes. Last week I went back to a basketball memory. In eighth grade I practiced with the boys' basketball team because we didn't have a girls' team. The coach was impossible; the boys ridiculed me and my best friend; I kept going. I want to write this story, and since there are no assignments in writing group, I can write whatever is on my mind. I do.

I drop a draft in the mailboxes of the five group regulars and save a few for guests that drop in irregularly. We rarely have more than four at a meeting each week. We read one another's work and write notes about our connections, our questions, and our interest in the piece. There's a crackling energy in the room as we ping one idea off another.

"The scene you wrote at the window was amazing. I could see your grandma in the yard, like a ghost, missing her the way you did."

"But the heart of the piece—is it your anger at God for her death?"

"Is it the regret you're wrestling with for going to camp that summer?"

Julie's written about losing her grandmother ten years ago, and we all find lines we love, things we want to know more about, and ways that her experience helps us understand our own. We share ideas and wonderings, not judgments. I always leave writing group wanting to write more.

Home at night I find the draft I'm working on and look at the notes my writing friends have left me. They ask hard questions. They encourage me to keep slugging. I take their ideas and run—creating words and scenes as my fingers dance like twin spiders across the keyboard.

"You're up late," my husband says. "Are you writing?"

"I'm trying," I say, "just give me ten more minutes."

An hour disappears.

This romance with language and ideas and the power of writing bleeds into my classroom the next morning. I want to share with my students, as Jane Kenyon says, "how hard it is to write, how hard it is to know what you want to say and to say what you mean" (Moyers 1995, 223). I want to show my students where I am in my draft and where I want it to be. Some days I do show them and our talk is rich, real: those indelible moments in teaching that burn like the sun.

I speak differently to students on those mornings after writing group. They can feel it. Mem Fox said,

> Teachers of writing who have been soldiers themselves, engaged in
> a writing battle, must be able to empathize more closely with the
> comrades in their classroom than teachers who are merely war
> correspondents at the hotel bar, as it were, watching the battle from
> a safe distance, declining to get in there themselves and write.
> (1993, 11)

I know how hard it can be to make words line up the way you want them to. It isn't because I didn't try hard enough or didn't "revise." I'm thinking as hard as I can some days and the piece still reads like a bad cut-and-paste job. I give my students what my writing friends give me: honest response, genuine encouragement, a few suggestions, and energy to keep writing what matters.

My students respond with better writing. They invest in their drafts because I invest in mine. Our momentum grows—*try this—how did you do that?*—during workshop. A spontaneous standing ovation erupted last week after a student read a story that we had nurtured through successive drafts. We are writers—we rock together.

I'm back to writing group the next week with my revisions in hand. Maybe I only found a spare thirty minutes to work on the piece that week, but I try a few things, keep working at it, and we talk about what else is possible in my story—what lies beneath what I've written. My best ideas come from these people. My mind spins. Within the possibilities that appear for this one narrative I'm working on are the many ideas I will offer in class that week. I see more, I understand more, I share more. One experience feeds the other in joyful harmony—a blend of voices: mine, my writing group, my students.

Carrie brings in draft four of "Seven Years and Not a Decent Cord of Wood," her ode to a former boyfriend. It is crafty and hilarious and so Carrie. We cheer each addition and snicker at relationships gone bad. I become determined to memorialize my first love—somehow. It's a piece waiting for me when I return to my desk and stare in wonder at the blank page. Anything goes. What will the writing bring?

My writing group is the single most important professional development experience I've had as a teacher. No national conference compares, no book has taught me as much, no district workshop has ever had as big an impact on my daily growth as a teacher. Four or five teachers in a room with a few rough drafts create conversations that probe for meaning, that teach the process from the inside. Although the writing is recursive—one draft becomes another piece entirely, a revision leads back to a former draft—this experience of writing with others creates a forward momentum that drives me to learn. I discover how writing works. I uncover what to teach. I determine how to sustain energy when January's days begin and end in darkness and the temperature won't climb above zero. Writers notice more, sing more, laugh more. We live more deeply in community with one another and the student writers in our room. That's a pretty big paycheck for an hour a week.

🦋

USING CONVENTIONS

Everything a writer does is an act of convention. My words go from left to right on the page; I put spaces between them; I try to use correct spellings, punctuation, capitalization, and grammar. These conventions are a contract between me the writer and you the reader. I care enough about my text that I don't want to confuse you.

I am my own first reader. I mark off the meaning of the text so that I don't confuse myself. I work hard to be clear. I show more than I tell. I identify the heartbeat, the main part of the text where I show most clearly what I mean. I supply evidence, details, that back up my claims and assertions. Once I feel that my meaning is clear I go back and doublecheck my conventions.

Some writers attend closely to conventions as they go along. Others tumble through their drafts more roughly and fix them up when they reread and rework them.

SEE DON REREADING HIS DRAFT FOR CONVENTIONS IN USING CONVENTIONS: "DON'S DEMONSTRATION."

Evaluators who read children's work on tests review the conventions they are using. I may be speaking out of turn, but most evaluators attend to conventions first, because if the writer hasn't taken the pains to attend to marking off the text, the evaluator immediately infers, "This author doesn't care about me."

Teachers work very hard in their classrooms to build an atmosphere of respect for others, and this in turn extends to students' writing. Part of this respect is using the necessary conventions so that the reader—likely someone else at another place and time—will understand what has been written.

Children do not suddenly arrive at an understanding of conventions. The accurate use of conventions is a lifelong pursuit. Above all, I want an active text that is respectful of my readers. I want to be engaging, use common sense, and provide useful information.

AN APPROACH TO TEACHING CONVENTIONS

Here are some helpful principles.

1. Use your own writing to show how conventions help convey meaning.

SUE ANN HAS STUDENTS STUDY HER CONVENTIONS CHOICES IN USING CONVENTIONS: "A CONVENTIONS MINILESSON."

2. Teach only one or two conventions at a time. Teach them well and make sure children apply them to their own texts.

3. Present at least three examples of the use of a convention during a minilesson.

4. Keep a running list in the classroom of conventions taught during minilessons. Expect all students to attend to these conventions.

5. Ask students to pass in a paragraph once a week in which they have applied writing conventions to the best of their ability. Have them circle words they think may be misspelled and put boxes around punctuation they suspect may not be correct.

6. Have students practice underlining the first five verbs and the first five nouns in the piece.

I want children to be conscious of the conventions they already know. As an example, I write a text on an overhead.

> I was sitting watching TV when I spotted a red fox out the window and running up the road. He turned, went across the street, and jumped up on a rock. His ears were pointing straight up. I raced to get my camera and went outside shooting away. When I came back in the house my wife said the fox came over to them and then walked down into the trees. All I could think of was, "What if I'd been standing with them? What great shots I might have gotten!" ❦

I post four categories of conventions on the chalkboard or a transparency—general conventions, punctuation, spelling, and grammar—and ask the children which conventions I've used. They usually come up with:

GENERAL CONVENTIONS: Writing from left to right, putting spaces between words, writing lines went from top to bottom, putting capitals at the beginning of sentences.

PUNCTUATION: Using periods, question marks, exclamation points, and quotation marks; using a comma to separate items in a series.

SPELLING: Words generally look accurate; are there two *ns* or only one in *running*? Draw a line under the word and check it later.

GRAMMAR: I have one problem here. Can you spot it? Who is *them?* Pronouns are tough. *Them* doesn't refer to anyone. I never mentioned that a friend was standing with my wife.

Then I issue an invitation: For today I'd like you to do a quick write on one animal you have seen in the woods, the park, or the street. Write rapidly for five minutes, stop, put in conventions you think you know, then hand the paper in with your list. Just focus on the first two categories: general conventions and punctuation.

The following day I ask the children to take the same piece and underline the words they are certain are spelled correctly. Next, they circle the words they are not sure are spelled correctly. Learning to estimate what words are spelled correctly is important work because the ability to estimate is the beginning of learning. (I'll say more about spelling later.)

THE CONVENTION GAME

About fifteen years ago I developed a game in which children in elementary school learn approximately twenty-five conventions for punctuation in their own texts as well as in the books they are reading. Here's how I introduce the game.

"We are going to start a new game today; I call it the convention game. You'll be working in teams. You'll need to bring your writing folder and the book you are reading in order to play. So, move your desks and chairs together. You'll need to be close to each other in order to talk quickly and quietly." I quickly assign heterogeneous teams of three students each, avoiding any impression of obvious deliberation about who should work together.

I continue. "This is the way the game is played. I will put a sentence up on the board that shows a particular convention and I'll underline it. That's the one I want you to find in your folder or book." I write the sentence, *There are many kinds of whales: blue whales, humpback whales, sperm whales, and right whales.* (The game moves quickly if you have the sentences with underlined conventions written out on a transparency before you begin.) "Notice that I've underlined this mark here, the colon. All right, teams, go to work. First, look at your papers in the writing folder, and if you can't find a colon there, look in your books. The minute someone finds it, he or she says, 'I've got one.' Immediately, the rest of the team members look to be sure it's really a colon. Your next job is to talk over these important questions: How does this convention help the meaning of the sentence? How does this help readers?

"Take this group of boys here, Robbie, Mark, and Daryl. Maybe Robbie finds it in his book, but Daryl is able to come up with how it best helps the meaning of the sentence. Daryl's job is to teach Robbie and Mark. When everyone in the group thinks they know how it helps the meaning, all three boys put their hands up. Unless I see three hands I won't count a team as ready."

This point often needs to be reiterated. Children are so used to solo learning that the child who finds the convention and knows its use raises his hand, ignoring his partners. Or, two members of a group will get it and not teach the third member who is having a hard time understanding. When this happens I say, "I can see two hands up, but by the look on Robbie's face he wants you two to do a better job of teaching him."

When three groups of students have their hands up, I stop and call on a member of the team who had their hands up first. "All right, Robbie, what's the convention and how does it help us understand this sentence better?" I can call on any member of a group to answer. I don't need to know who found the convention or who first understood its meaning.

"All right, let's do another one." I write the sentence, *I can't decide whether I like pizza with pepperoni, mushrooms, or sausage.* "Notice where I've underlined. Now see if you can find a structure like that." I wait.

"All right we now have three groups with their hands up. I'll call on you, Janet, from your team. What is the convention and how does it help the meaning?"

Janet says, "Well, the commas separate the different pizzas. It organizes the sentence better."

"Good thinking. The commas do help organize the sentence. They also create a pause for the reader."

I then call on a member of each of the other two groups before putting another example on the board.

"Okay, from now on the credit is going to go this way. If your team finds the convention in your own writing it counts for two points; if it's in the book you are reading, you get only one point."

I play the game for ten or fifteen minutes every couple of weeks because it heightens students' awareness of punctuation conventions.

EXPERIMENTING WITH NOUNS AND VERBS

There are two very important parts of speech I wish to teach in any grade—verbs and nouns. Nouns are *stuff*—material, people, or places. I compose a piece of writing and interpolate the appropriate dialogue.

> *I like to go to the mall.* Can you tell the name of a place or thing in what I just wrote? Yes, it is *mall*, and that's a place. We call that a noun. Let's underline it. *I just walk along and look in the windows.* Are there any things in that sentence? Yes, *windows*. What kinds of things might we see in the store windows? Okay, *electronics, clothes, sports equipment.* Let's choose sports. What do you see in the sports window? *I see snow boards, ski poles, skis, weights, barbells, shoes.* Every one of these is a noun: you can pick them up. Try one more window, clothes. *I see sweaters, belts, shoes, jewelry.* All those items I

see in the window are nouns. *I also see clerks waiting on customers.* Tell me what the nouns are in that last sentence. Yes, we move from things to people, *clerks* and *customers*. *Clerks* and *customers* are also nouns. All right, take your piece and underline the nouns. Then pass in your paper.

I'll work on nouns for two straight days, moving to abstract nouns like *law, justice, religion.*

On another day I'll work with verbs. I write another piece to show what I mean.

Basketball is one of my favorite sports. Can you tell the two nouns here? *There is so much action in basketball. I like to focus on one player. I like to watch him move and play.* Tell me what action words there are in that last sentence. Yes, there's *watch, move,* and *play.* There's another more difficult one: *like.* You can't really see *like* the way you can see the other actions. But *I* is followed by an action, *like. I want, I wish, I have. Want, wish,* and *have* are all verbs. You don't see the action as you do with *move* and *play.* I'll continue to write. *I follow my man when he dribbles, shoots, passes, or jumps for a rebound.* Tell me the verbs here. Yes, *follow, dribbles, shoots, passes,* and *jumps* are all verbs.

I do several follow-up lessons, no longer than five or ten minutes, on verbs. I ask the students to examine their work for obvious verbs. When I ask students to underline the first five verbs in their writing, they need to know what they are, as well as how to make them more precise and vivid.

Sometimes I ask a student to show me a better action than the one she has on the page. *I wore the blouse* is not as precise as *I thrust my arm into the sleeve, all the while feeling the fit on my shoulder and glancing at the look of the blouse in the mirror.* Break down the action into component verbs or a more precise nature. Slow the action down.

CHANGING THE CULTURE
SURROUNDING THE TEACHING
OF SPELLING

Forty-five percent of English words are spelled the way they sound. Fifty-five percent of English words require the writer to draw on visual memory systems. There is no correlation between spelling and intelligence. A third of the U.S. population can't spell, and another 10 to 15 percent have certain bugaboo words that cause them to consider themselves poor spellers. A self-diagnosed poor speller tends to avoid writing or, worse, doesn't want to reread because he knows he can't identify most of his misspellings. Poor spellers are punished on examinations, tests, and, in general, schoolwork.

How can we change the culture surrounding poor spellers and marginal spellers? We cannot ignore poor spelling. First, we have to focus on the message in the writing. When I attend to the child's knowing, respond to details in his message, the child knows that I know he knows something. Second, we want other children to acknowledge his knowing. If I can get a child to care about his information as well as his audience, this opens the door to caring about his piece.

Computers help. First, almost all word-processing programs have a spell-check feature. In addition, the child gets a clear visual image of the piece from the machine-printed text. Poor handwriting often contributes to poor spelling simply because the child has an inconsistent visual image of the words. Of course, when children take tests on their writing skills, computers are not available.

I give students credit for sensing when a word may be misspelled. Students usually do well on words that are linked to images: *baseball, football, dinosaur, ballet* (even though *ballet* is a French word, it is a prestigious word). Unfortunately, words like *when, which, where,* or *their* don't have images associated with them and are commonly misspelled.

Cindy Marten takes an intelligent approach to spelling in her book *Word Crafting* (2003). She goes beyond spelling lists of words learned in isolation to keeping lists of words that cause problems for the particular student. Students proofread their own texts. Thus spelling is used in the *service* of writing.

Spelling matters. Probably more than any other part of the school curriculum, spelling affects a student's social status. The American public still sees good spelling just behind reading and mathematics in importance. Children who initially write down words using inventions or temporary spellings are establishing learning habits and attitudes toward words and writing. As arbitrary as spelling may appear, specific things should be taught and certain attitudes established and early. It is not enough for the writer to know what the text says, the reader needs to know as well. Writing is communication.

In spite of all I know about learning to spell, I'll admit that when something one of my daughters writes contains misspellings, I itch. I want the unsightly word removed. In my knee-jerk response, I overlook the message. I am objective about the misspellings of others, but within my family? What will other people think?

Experienced administrators and teachers know that they need good data on spelling progress. In today's political climate, poor spelling makes parents and school board members forget other successes in the school curriculum. Of course, there is no correlation between spelling ability and intelligence (otherwise, we might lose a third of the people in law, teaching, and the medical professions). As Harold Rosen so delightfully says: "Any idiot can tell a genius how to spell a word."

Young children don't suddenly spell correctly any more than they begin to speak perfectly. When Betty and my first child pointed a crooked finger at a bird and my daughter spoke her first word, *bir,* we nearly wept with joy. We raced inside to tell my mother. We didn't pull our ten-month-old aside and say, "After us, Marion, let's say all of it, get that final *d.*" It was enough of a miracle to hear her first word. Naturally, as she grew older her vocabulary expanded; and if she had continued to drop the final consonant in later years, we probably would have worked with her on it.

When I refer to *inventive spelling,* a term first used by Carol Chomsky (1971), I mean the spellings children formulate before they know the full conventional spelling of a word. Children usually approximate the full spelling by writing the word down by the way it sounds. Many researchers have shown how these spellings evolve from just the consonants to later include vowels. Inventive spelling allows children to begin to make meaning before they know how to spell a word. However, by the upper elementary years, students should be spelling most words conventionally. All students should be encouraged to spell words correctly, even when drafting, so that the writer can concentrate on the flow of her ideas and not be preoccupied with accuracy at the early stage of a draft. I expect to see a growing improvement over time in first-draft spelling and the use of conventions. More and more conventions and spellings should become automatic. If I do not see an improvement, I need to speak with the student to help her focus more on what she is learning.

FREQUENTLY USED WORDS

Children need to know how to read and spell certain common words (see the table on p. 94). These words can be posted on a word wall in the classroom or pasted into a writing folder. These are not the easiest words for children to learn, even though most of them are short. Most do not lend themselves to imagery, and therefore they need to be taught in the context of reading and writing.

SPELLING TESTS AND PERSONAL WORD LISTS

The traditional weekly spelling lists commonly found in published spelling books in connection with Monday-to-Friday skills exercises have a bleak history. Cohen (in Graves 1977) shows that calling

The Instant Words* First Hundred

These are the most common words in English, ranked in frequency order. The first 25 make up about a third of all printed material. The first 100 make up about half of all written material. Is it any wonder that all students must learn to recognize these words instantly and to spell them correctly also?

Words 1–25	Words 26–50	Words 51–75	Words 76–100
the	or	will	number
of	one	up	no
and	had	other	way
a	by	about	could
to	word	out	people
in	but	many	my
is	not	then	than
you	what	them	first
that	all	these	water
it	were	so	been
he	we	some	call
was	when	her	who
for	your	would	oil
on	can	make	now
are	said	like	find
as	there	him	long
with	use	into	down
his	an	time	day
they	each	has	did
I	which	look	get
at	she	two	come
be	do	more	made
this	how	write	may
have	their	go	part
from	if	see	over

Common suffixes: -s, -ing, -ed

* For additional instant words, see *Spelling Book* by Edward Fly, Laguna Beach Educational Books, 245 Grandview, Laguna Beach CA 92651 (1992).

The NEW Reading Teacher's Book of Lists, ©1985 Prentice Hall, Inc. Englewood Cliffs, NJ 07632. By E. Fry, D. Fountoukidis, and J. Polk.

attention to word parts, phonetic respellings, dictionary skills, and so on actually causes children's spelling ability to regress. Cohen's research shows quite clearly that using words in children's own writing is the strongest contributor to spelling power.

Spelling lists are effective if students keep an ongoing list of the words they use frequently. The list can be kept in the writing folder and added to each week when misspelled words are encountered in the student's writing. The student then studies and practices these words. Nancie Atwell documents her approach to learning five personalized words a week in *Lessons That Change Writers* (Atwell 2002).

Some classrooms create class dictionaries for students to consult when they need help spelling a word. Sometimes these are *pictionaries,* which include a drawing beside the word. This type of reference is particularly helpful for children who are weak on sound–letter correspondence, especially those learning English as a second language. (A caveat: verbs are more difficult to illustrate than are nouns.)

Clearly, the child who reads a great deal sees words spelled correctly more often and will develop a personal word bank of words they recall when writing. Reading provides both an image and a clear visual memory of what a word looks like. Some good readers have a way of noticing details that help them remember word spellings. Conversely, some very good readers do not take in the visual features of a word and continue to have a difficult time with spelling.

STRATEGIES TO HELP WRITERS WITH SPELLING

When writers care about a piece and have an audience in mind (beyond the teacher), you are in the best position to help them with their spelling. Students who don't care about their writing or have no idea of what writing can do are the most difficult to help. Teachers work hard to find out how a student's energy can be channeled into something she cares about. When her voice is in the piece, the author cares more about being respectful of those who will read her work.

Ask students to start at the end of their piece and read backward toward the beginning. It is easier to locate misspelled words this way because readers are less likely to be lulled by the meaning and skip over words. Have them circle words they think may be misspelled or that look strange to them. Your first step in working with poor spellers is to help them gain confidence in their ability to recognize misspellings: children who really struggle are convinced that it is a fruitless task. And even if they find a misspelled word, consulting a dictionary is tedious and difficult. It is important to help children see improvement in their ability to reread a text and find errors. Don't let poor spellers confuse ideas and intelligence with the ability to spell.

Sometimes parents only see the misspelled words; they don't see the progress toward correct spelling. They worry that their child will stick with approximate spellings. They need to see their child's progress and development. Parents reluctant to accept an idea in theory are receptive to practical evidence that their child is learning and growing. Use the child's writing to show this progress. As an example, one teacher took a writing folder containing a year's worth of writing, photocopied the pieces, and showed the parents how their child's spelling changed during the year.

⁑

IN CONCLUSION

You have now completed the first step of your journey inside writing. You have experimented with narrative, poetry, essay, and fiction to create texts for your classroom demonstrations. You have discovered stories in responding to quick writes and have learned a few strategies that will lead you to a close revision of your work. As you continue to work with your writing, you will likely discover a new energy for teaching the writing process, and as your students watch writing develop through your demonstration lessons, they will gain a new vision for their own writing. This joyful exchange, writer to writer, will bring clarity and power to writing in all genres.

APPENDIX A

TEN FREQUENTLY ASKED QUESTIONS ABOUT QUICK WRITES

1. **I CAN'T FIND TIME FOR WRITING, SO HOW DO I FIND TIME FOR QUICK WRITES?**

   Often a classroom activity may not take quite as much time as you've allotted, leaving time for a quick write. Choose one of the quick writes from the accompanying *My Quick Writes* notebook, read it to the class, and watch what happens. Write along with them. When teachers are writing too, children are more focused. Assign a quick write on something your students have just experienced—yesterday's snowstorm, the fight on the playground during recess. Begin your writing workshop with a quick write.

2. **WHAT IS THE RELATIONSHIP BETWEEN A QUICK WRITE AND THE WRITING PROGRAM?**

   A quick write helps children get past thinking about *what* to write and get busy writing. It also begins to develop the writer's voice. After three or four quick writes, students lose their inhibitions and begin to sound more like themselves. Quick writes are not *the* writing program, but when they are liberally sprinkled throughout a month—eight or ten times, say—other kinds of writing becomes stronger. The accompanying notebook suggests quick writes in five different genres.

3. HOW WILL QUICK WRITES HELP MY STUDENTS ON STATE OR NATIONAL ASSESSMENTS?

Practicing quick writes will greatly improve students' ability to get to the heart of the topic, which is just what most assessments require. Writers also learn how to support their claims with details.

4. YOU CALL QUICK WRITES A BEGINNING LABORATORY FOR TEACHING WRITING. WHAT DO YOU MEAN BY THAT?

Quick writes are a way to experiment, a way to try things out. The basics of writing are all contained within a short piece of writing. Most important, quick writes lend themselves to various rereadings, beginning with enjoying and appreciating what has been written and moving on to looking at the details. Much of writing is rereading, and many children are never taught how to reread their work. It's important that they become comfortable doing so.

5. WHAT IS THE BEST WAY FOR STUDENTS TO MARK UP AND ARCHIVE THEIR QUICK WRITES?

Some teachers give their students a spiral-bound notebook just for quick writes. Others have their students store their quick writes in a folder. It's helpful if students are able to mark different features of the text with different-colored pencils.

6. SOME STUDENTS DRAW A BLANK WHEN I READ THE QUICK-WRITE PROMPT. HOW CAN I HELP THEM?

Some quick writes just don't connect with a particular student. Or, a writer may have something else on her mind that day. Make sure students understand that a prompt can lead in many directions to many topics. Stress the idea of *options* and that it's okay to borrow another student's idea: one student writes about his dog, so the student next to him writes about *his* dog.

7. WHY SHOULD I DO THE SAME QUICK WRITE AS MY STUDENTS?

When students see you perform the act of writing, they become engaged in their own writing. Also, students are very curious about *what* you are writing. Writing is communication. They want to know more about you as a human being. You don't have to show your students a copy of your text. You can just read it aloud when everyone is sharing. Teachers often ask me, "But won't the students be discouraged by my writing? Or won't they copy my topic?" Not at all. They are amazed to see a teacher write, because teachers rarely do write in this capacity. You may be the very first teacher they've seen write.

8. WHAT'S THE BEST WAY FOR STUDENTS TO SHARE THEIR QUICK WRITES?

Sometimes I have students share a few words, phases, or sentences they like from their pieces. Students may add why they chose these parts, but they don't have to. Occasionally, they may share an entire piece. In that case, I expect the audience to respond in a specific way: (1) what they remember, (2) what they were struck by, and (3) one or two questions they have.

9. GOOD FICTION IS QUITE DIFFICULT FOR MY STUDENTS TO WRITE. HOW CAN I KEEP THEM FROM GETTING BOGGED DOWN IN LAST NIGHT'S STALE TV PLOT?

Television fiction is often the worst kind of fiction. TV producers know that if there isn't fast-moving action, they'll lose their audiences. It becomes caricature. Basically, fiction is all about character. A prompt that encourages good solid dialogue may be the way in, so experiment!

10. YOU SAY STUDENTS CAN DO QUICK WRITES IN ANY GENRE. DON'T I HAVE TO TEACH THE GENRE FIRST?

You should first demonstrate some of the basics of the genre with your own writing. Also, help students be aware of specific things to look for when rereading each genre. The most important thing is to encourage experimentation in the genre by showing your own attempts with topics that matter to you.

TEMPLATE FOR TAKING NOTES DURING WRITING CONFERENCES

TITLE/TOPIC	CONF DATE _____	SHARE DATE _____	FINAL SAY DATE _____
TITLE/TOPIC	CONF DATE _____	SHARE DATE _____	FINAL SAY DATE _____
TITLE/TOPIC	CONF DATE _____	SHARE DATE _____	FINAL SAY DATE _____
TITLE/TOPIC	CONF DATE _____	SHARE DATE _____	FINAL SAY DATE _____
TITLE/TOPIC	CONF DATE _____	SHARE DATE _____	FINAL SAY DATE _____

SAMPLE TEACHER NOTES ON WRITING CONFERENCES

Title / topic	Conf date	Share date	Final say date
Dog Story		9/20 With Jenna—telling her to listen for the exciting part. Good feedback from J. on action.	10/2 She's proud of this. Great experiments in dialogue—learning those mechanics too. Still—it's hard to follow. Needs work on organizing
Newsletter Piece	10/7 Discussed +practiced turning her interview notes into newspiece		
New Kid In School Story	10/22 Slow getting started on her story board. Seemed to get idea from Read Aloud—TooManyCats. Push her to zoom in on the heartbeat moments.	10/24 With M. sharing their storyboards. Some good feedback—asked her questions about the setting.	11/5 Super editing! Organization better w/ storyboard. Still few details—little sense of audience.
Rainstorm Poem	11/3 Showed me very short draft. Showed her some poems with sensory language. So she's excited to include sounds, smells, slips, etc.		11/10 Fun line breaks. Sensory language works.
		A small Post It note can fit in this space for notes taken on the run.	

Appendix D

Developing a Quick Write into A Personal Narrative

❧

"Basketball Dreams"
First Draft

Just do it.
—Nike slogan

The cement wall was cold against my head and neck and my legs crossed, uncrossed, stretched and bunched up. I pulled my long, blonde hair back into a pony tail.

"David." Kirk said it with authority; he always picked him first. The repetition was reliable at least: every day Kirk and Bobby were captains, David and Alan were first picks.

"Alan."

See? Told you.

There was barely a pause as Keith–Aaron–John–Matt–Billy–Eddy and even fat, uncoordinated Ron jumped off the bench to form two packs of boys with their captains at the center of the basketball court eyeing the two girls that were left. I hated this part. More than cold lima beans on my plate at dinner or scraping wax off of our hardwood floors at home, I hated this choosing teams thing. Just once, I wanted to be captain. I'd leave Kirk and Bobby for last.

No I wouldn't, actually.

"Time Somebody Told Me"
"Flaws?"

20 Oct 04

basketball memories...   5 minutes

The cement wall was cold against my
head and neck and my legs crossed, *I pulled my long blonde hair back into a pony tail.*
uncrossed, stretched and bunched up.

Every day Kirk & "David." Kirk always picked him first.
Bobby were captains. David & Alan were first picks.
"Alan." Bobby went next.
See? I told you.
There was Barely a pause as Keith. Aaron. John.
Matt. Billy. Eddy. and even Ron jumped
off the bench to form two packs of
boys with their captains at the center *of the basketball*
eyeing ~~what was~~ *the two girls that were* left. I hated this *court*
part. More than green peas or cold
mashed potatoes for lunch, I hated
choosing teams. Just once I wanted to be captain.
~~As the bench emptied~~ Julie and I
Kirk coughed and said, sat side-by-side waiting for ~~the end.~~ *it to be over.*
~~Always,~~ "Julie." with a *resigned* sigh, then Bobby let
~~I guess~~ we'll take Penny. " *he said a* *there be a long pause- long enough for me*
groan and *out of the boys* rolled eyes. all around. *then*
Mr. Nelson said, "overtures play." It was hard to be ~~the only two girls~~ *one of two girls* *to sit alone on that bench.*
on the junior high boys' basketball team. *camera to his cheeks.*
I don't know why I kept going. Our *to practice.* *why I quit?*
P.E. teacher, Mr. Nelson, didn't want us ove

NOTE BOOK

Oct. 20 Belle-Isle's class

first he laughed and said girls didn't play on
the boys' team; it was ridiculous.
the team. ~~Somebody made him~~ letting us
practice every morning at 7:30, ~~but~~ We
changed in the dark because Mr Nelson he kept
clothes
in the girls locker room. forgetting to turn the lights on
~~or us.~~ I don't think he forgot.
We asked if we could be captains. He
said, "That's ridiculous. You're girls."
      asked
Julie ~~said~~, "Just once?" but she
kept her eyes on the floor and when he
didn't answer we just went to class.
   Our first home game was against
Wilson Elementary. We showed up early
with the rest of the team, but Mr. Nelson
didn't have uniforms for us. He said
there weren't enough. I didn't believe him. I
still don't. (TP) Title IX arrived & stopped that discrimination.
   And in the 30 years that separate that
                   my childhood and the present day
moment form now, we have technology and cheap
international travel, but that teacher habit that
never worked for more than a few kids remains.

then Julie's dad said something to the principal and he starred

My daughter could play on a girls' team if she chose to i but

the piece I wrote about choosing up sides in XC practice or gym class	And Kids are still being hurt by it — in classrooms and at practice, choosing teams can be unhealthy.

Winning was everything.

And they were the cutest, most popular boys in eighth grade.

Julie and I sat side by side waiting. Kirk coughed and said, "Julie," with a resigned sigh. Fair pick; she was better. Bobby just looked at the wall. He let there be a long pause, long enough for me to sit alone on that bench, color coming to my cheeks. Why did I like this boy?

"I guess we'll take Penny," he said with a groan.

All of my "teammates" rolled their eyes.

Mr. Johnson jumped in with, "Okay boys, let's practice," firing basketballs onto the court from the rolling cart.

I don't know why I kept going. First our coach laughed when we asked about try-outs. He said, "Girls don't play on the boys' team; that's ridiculous."

Julie and I kept practicing night after night at the hoop in front of her house. We played in darkness, rain and too early in the morning for the neighbors, but our game was something. There wasn't a girl in the school who came close. But it was 1974 and there wasn't a girls' team at our school; our only hope was the boys'.

Julie's dad said something to the principal and he started letting us practice every morning at 7:30. No one liked it. The coach fumed. We changed our clothes in the dark because he kept forgetting to turn the lights in the girls' locker room. The boys elbowed us away from the basket and argued over who had to guard us.

It was miserable, but we were stubborn.

We asked if we could be captains for one practice. Coach Johnson said, "That's ridiculous," like it was intended as a joke and he winked at us, until he realized we weren't kidding. He sobered up. "You're girls," as if that explained something. I'm not sure who I hated more: him or me: being a girl and athletic felt like a terminal disease.

Julie persisted, "Just once?" and he glared at her long and hard. She kept her eyes on the floor and when he didn't answer, we just went to sit on the bench again.

Our first home game was against Wilson Elementary. We showed up early with the rest of the team, but Mr. Johnson didn't have uniforms for us. He said there weren't enough. I didn't believe him. He told us we couldn't sit on the bench in street clothes, but we could watch in the stands. I felt tears. I cursed my every weakness.

I watched the team lose.

·L

WHAT NEXT?

I can't figure out what to do next because I don't know why I'm writing the piece . . . What am I try to say? . . . Why does this story matter to me?

- It could be about athletics in my life—and how my love for basketball in junior high led to being a four-year varsity letterman in tennis—determination in the face of every possible obstacle with Mr. Johnson led me to fight really hard for my place on every athletic team after.

- It could be about junior high—another story of struggling to fit in and feeling like I never would.

- It could be about teachers like Mr. Johnson who are mean and small and made my life miserable—and why after all that did I become a teacher anyway?

- It could be about basketball as an escape from home—a reason to be away as much as possible during those difficult adolescent years.

·L

ENDING WORK . . .

I first have to commit to working on this. I don't want to because I like what I've written so far and I don't want to spoil it. As Kim Stafford says in *The Muses Among Us,* "It's a tough truth that drafts often get worse in revision, before they get better. This is natural. The first genius had a shine that may be tarnished by revision. There is a clear lawn, then the messy digging that begins a garden, then the order of the garden when it flourishes" (2003, 37). Revision always requires faith that messing it up will make it better.

HOW TO START?

I know I want to capture a scene from one of my experiences playing sports in high school to show my drive to win built from basketball dreams. I'm thinking of tennis because I loved it most. To write the scene I have to reread the draft and then start.

> Years later I drove across town with my mother to pick up my letterman's sweater. It was ivory with maroon lining in the pockets. Mom sewed the large "F" on that night and I added in patches for each of the sports I lettered in: tennis, cheerleading, gymnastics. The most satisfying moment, though, was peeling off the ivory strips on the left sleeve. There were four maroon stripes buried there and I peeled off every one: I was a four-year varsity letterman. Mr. Johnson taught me to work harder for what I wanted. He eroded my confidence in basketball, but my hunger to win remained.
>
> As it does today. *&

FIRST TRY: I hate it. If I decide to use it, I have to spend more time stretching out this scene so readers become involved in it.

SECOND TRY: I'll go with "teachers like Mr. Johnson who are mean and small and miserable and why did I become a teacher anyway?"

I moved from eighth grade to high school where my drive to win earned me a spot as a freshman on a competitive varsity tennis team. I played at the bottom of the roster behind girls who'd grown up at tennis clubs and tennis camps: I saw the distance between us. I kept at it. I served hundreds of balls once practice was over each afternoon; I read books on strategy and challenged the best girl over and over, trying to learn how she beat me.

It was more than precision and strength; she just knew she could.

Mr. Johnson eroded my confidence in basketball with his steady assault on my ability. I didn't try out for the girls' team in high school: I believed I wasn't good enough. He left an even more corrosive mark on my spirit. It took years of winning to quiet the familiar growl in my ear, the sneer that chased me across the court each morning as an awkward 13-year-old.

When I became a teacher and a coach I vowed to never be mean and small and miserable.

I win that one for my students. 🏃

I like this one better. Now I can move on to polishing.

REFERENCES

Atwell, Nancie. 2002. *Lessons That Change Writers.* Portsmouth, NH: Heinemann.

Chomsky, Carol Schatz. 1971. *The Acquisition of Syntax in Children from 5 to 10.* Cambridge, MA: MIT Press.

Fox, Mem. 1993. *Radical Reflections: Passionate Opinions on Teaching, Learning, and Living.* New York: Harcourt.

Graves, D. H. 1973. "Children's Writing: Research Directions and Hypotheses Based upon an Examination of the Writing Process of Seven Year Old Children." Ann Arbor, MI.

———. 1977. "Spelling Texts and Structural Analysis Methods." *Language Arts* 54(1).

———. 1989. *Experiment with Fiction.* The Reading/Writing Teacher's Companion. Portsmouth, NH: Heinemann.

———. 1989. *Investigate Nonfiction.* The Reading/Writing Teacher's Companion. Portsmouth, NH: Heinemann.

———. 1992. *Explore Poetry.* The Reading/Writing Teacher's Companion. Portsmouth, NH: Heinemann.

———. 1994. *A Fresh Look at Writing.* Portsmouth, NH: Heinemann.

Karelitz, E. B. 1993. *The Author's Chair and Beyond.* Portsmouth, NH: Heinemann.

Kittle, P. 2003. *Public Teaching: One Kid at a Time.* Portsmouth, NH: Heinemann.

Marten, C. 2003. *Word Crafting: Teaching Spelling, Grades K–6.* Portsmouth, NH: Heinemann.

Moyers, Bill. 1995. *The Language of Life: A Festival of Poets.* New York: Broadway Books.

Murray, Donald M. 2003. *A Writer Teaches Writing, Revised Second Edition.* Boston: Heinle.

Rief, Linda. 2003. *100 Quick Writes.* New York: Scholastic.

Simon, N. 1992. "The Art of the Theatre No. 10." *Paris Review* 125 (winter).

Stafford, Kim. 2003. *The Muses Among Us: Eloquent Listening and Other Pleasures of the Writer's Craft.* Athens, GA: University of Georgia Press.

Vygotsky, L. S. 1962. *Thought and Language.* Cambridge, MA: MIT Press.